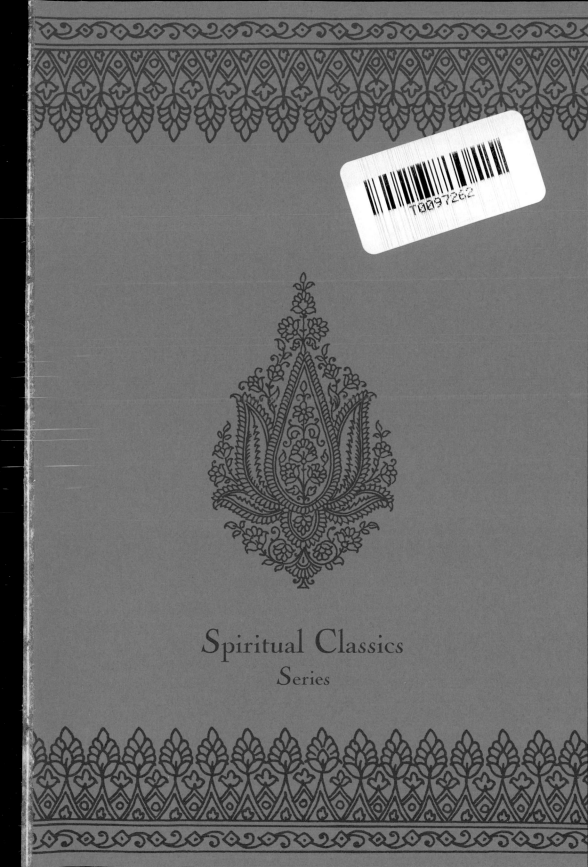

Spiritual Classics
Series

About this Book

on Lamp of Non-Dual Knowledge
(Advaita Bodha Deepika)

"Advaita or non-dual philosophy is the most satisfactory explanation of man's relationship to the all-pervading cosmic consciousness. Its message of all-enveloping equality is the panacea to the ills of modern society.

"Right from the time of the Upanishads, through Adi Sankara to Ramana, great preceptors have written treatises on Advaita philosophy and its powerful instrument of Self-enquiry. The epitome of all these voluminous writings has been later condensed by Karapatra Swami into a book of twelve chapters called *Sri Advaita Bodha Deepika*, 'The Lamp of Non-Dual Knowledge.'

"This book contains the English translation of the first eight chapters of the original Sanskrit text. The last four chapters have never been found. The work is a beautiful and clear treatise on Advaita Vedanta: how ignorance is super-imposed on the non-dual Self (*Adhyaropa*), its removal (*apavada*), the means of accomplishing it (*sadhana*) consisting of various methodologies, annihilation of latencies (*vasanakhayam*), the play of the mind in projecting the individual self, the world and the personal God, and the significance of Self-enquiry as the perfect instrument leading to the extinction of mind and the dawning of Self-realization. This is a veritable manual of non-dual philosophy."

—**V. S. Ramanan**, President, Sri Ramanasramam, India

on Cream of Liberation
(Kaivalya Navaneeta)

"In language easy to understand, the author gives a remarkably clear exposition of the tenets of Advaita. Its English translation will serve to make it known to a larger circle of readers and thus extend its usefulness."

—**V. A. Devasenapathi**, Professor of Philosophy, University of Madras

"The philosophy of the Advaita school is beyond a doubt the most satisfactory exposition of the transcendental relationship between the human soul and cosmic consciousness. Its all-encompassing quality is the message that the world desperately needs today to put an end to all internecine differences.

"The Advaita philosophy is subtle and needs a sincere application by the student. In the past, the difficulty was compounded by the fact that the medium in which it was conveyed was generally classical Sanskrit, not known to the majority of the people. Only during the last four centuries have works in Tamil imparting Advaita philosophy begun to appear. Out of these thirty or more works, the best known is Tandavaraya Swami's *Kaivalya Navaneeta*, 'The Cream of Liberation.'

"The work is presented in the form of a discussion between an earnest student and an enlightened preceptor. The great merit of this book consists of the lucid manner in which the subtle and abstract principles of this school of philosophy are presented with a number of examples. There is no doubt that the earnest seeker who studies this scripture will get a lucid understanding of Advaita philosophy and have all lurking doubts and objections removed."

—**V. S. Ramanan**, President, Sri Ramanasramam, India

World Wisdom
The Library of Perennial Philosophy

The Library of Perennial Philosophy is dedicated to the exposition of the timeless Truth underlying the diverse religions. This Truth, often referred to as the *Sophia Perennis*—or Perennial Wisdom—finds its expression in the revealed Scriptures as well as the writings of the great sages and the artistic creations of the traditional worlds.

The Perennial Philosophy—and its fundamental idea of the Religion of the Heart—provides the intellectual principles capable of explaining both the formal contradictions and the underlying unity of the great religions.

Ranging from the writings of the great sages who have expressed the *Sophia Perennis* in the past, to the perennialist authors of our time, each series of our Library has a different focus. As a whole, they express the inner unanimity, transforming radiance, and irreplaceable values of the great spiritual traditions.

Lamp of Non-Dual Knowledge & Cream of Liberation appears as one of our selections in The Spiritual Classics series.

Spiritual Classics Series

This series includes seminal, but often neglected, works of unique spiritual insight from leading religious authors of both the East and West. Ranging from books composed in ancient India to forgotten jewels of our time, these important classics feature new introductions which place them in the perennialist context.

Lamp of Non-Dual Knowledge

&

Cream of Liberation

Two Jewels of Indian Wisdom

Lamp of Non-Dual Knowledge is a translation of
Advaita Bodha Deepika by Sri Karapatra Swami.

Cream of Liberation is a translation of *Kaivalya Navaneeta,*
an ancient Tamil classic by Tandavaraya Swami.

Translations into English by
Swami Sri Ramanananda Saraswathi

World Wisdom

Lamp of Non-Dual Knowledge
&
Cream of Liberation

The text, Foreword, Preface to the 1965 Edition and Introductions,
appendices and index of *Lamp of Non-Dual Knowledge*
published by arrangement with V.S. Ramanan,
President, Board of Trustees,
Sri Ramanasramam, Tiruvannamalai 606 603.
All rights reserved.

Preface, the index of *Cream of Liberation* and Glossary
© 2003 World Wisdom, Inc.

Library of Congress Cataloging-in-Publication Data

Hariharânandasarasvatî, Swami
  [Advaita bodha dîpika. English]
  Lamp of non-dual knowledge : cream of liberation ; two jewels of
Indian wisdom ; translations of Advaita bodha deepika and Kaivalya
navaneeta by Tandavaraya Swami ; translated into English by Swami Sri
Ramanananda Saraswathi.
      p. cm.
Includes index.
  ISBN 0-941532-38-0 (Paperback : alk. paper)
  1. Advaita–Early works to 1800. I. Ramanananda Saraswathi, Swami.
II. Tântavarâya Cuvâmikal, 1408-1534. Kaivalliya navanîtam.
English. III. Title.
  B132.A3 H355
  181'.482–dc21

                                                                    2003001396

Printed on acid-free paper in Canada

For information address World Wisdom, Inc.
P.O. Box 2682, Bloomington, Indiana 47402-2682

www.worldwisdom.com

Table of Contents

Preface

In the *Chândogya-Upanishad* the wise Uddâlâka speaks the following words to his son: "That which is the subtle essence, this whole world has that essence for its Self. That is the Real. That is the Self. That art thou, Shvetaketu."

These words, echoing from the ancient well of Indian wisdom, proclaim the most profound message of the *Vedânta*: *Tat tvam asi* ("That art thou"). The *Vedântic* perspective finds its equivalents in the great religions; however, it is particularly direct and rendered with near mathematical precision in the following famous axiom of Shankara, which further clarifies the message of Uddâlâka to Shvetaketu: *"Brahma satyam jagan–mithya," "jîvo brahmaiva naparah"* (*Brahman* is real; the world is not real; the individual soul is non-different from *Brahman*). This axiom is the quintessence of the *advaita* (non-dual) doctrine which is implicit in the words of *Uddâlâka*. According to the *Upanishadic* tradition the *mahâvâkya* (great saying), *Tat tvam asi* ("That art thou") holds the seed of man's liberation from *samsâra* (the wheel of birth and death). It is a saving formula, revealed by Heaven, to teach man the true nature of his inmost self. Understood at the level where knowledge becomes being, this apparently simple formula opens the door to the highest realization of God.

How is this possible? What must man do to gain this realization? What are the necessary qualifications to embark upon the path to God? The answers to these questions and the elucidation of Uddâlâka's words form the central subject matter of both *Advaita Bodha Deepika* (*Lamp of Non-Dual Knowledge*) and *Kaivalya Navaneeta* (*Cream of Liberation*). Both books are highly concentrated distillations of the heart of *Advaita Vedânta*, presented through a series of questions and answers between Master and disciple. Opening these pages, the reader is transported back in time to a grassy spot under a shady tree outside a temple in south India to overhear a conversation concerning the most important questions of human existence.

Like many of the metaphysical treatises of ancient India the details regarding the history and composition of these books is quite sketchy. *Cream of Liberation* is more than five hundred years old and this is the only English translation from the Tamil. *Lamp of Non-Dual Knowledge,* also translated from Tamil, appears to be even older and, unfortunately, the last four chapters have been lost. The eight chapters translated here make numerous references to many of the most important scriptures, philosophical treatises on *advaita* and sages well-known to that tradition, including: *Brahma-Sûtras, Bhagavad-Gîtâ, Upanishads, Yoga-Vasishtha,* and the writings of both *Shankara* and *Vidyâranya.* It will be of additional interest to readers familiar with the *Vedântic* current, as it reached into the twentieth-century, that both books were recommended to all who desire liberation in the knowledge of God by Shri Ramana Maharshi (1879-1950), the world famous representative of "ancient and eternal India" and the "incarnation of what is primordial and incorruptible" in the spiritual tradition of that sub-continent.[1] For all serious seekers who wish to drink from the stream of the transforming wisdom that Hindus call *Sanâtana Dharma* ("Eternal Religion"), one cannot do better than start with books which were recommended by the great Bhagavân.

But let us return to the message of the *Chândogya-Upanishad*: *Tat tvam asi* ("That art thou"). *Vedânta* teaches that we can know because the profound knowledge of the Real is written in the very substance of our being. There is something profound in the human soul which identifies with God because there is something *of* the Reality of God residing in the center of the soul. This doctrine is repeated in the metaphysical doctrines of all religions. To quote from the famous fourteenth century Christian preacher and mystic, Meister Eckhart: "The soul is not like God: she is identical with him." And from a saying (*hadîth*)

---

1. Frithjof Schuon, *Language of the Self* (Bloomington: World Wisdom 1999).

of Muhammed, the Prophet of Islam: "He who knows himself verily knows his Lord."

According to the *Vedânta,* true freedom is not realized through the acquisition of power, fame or wealth. It is found in man's ability to de-individualize the ego and to see himself *sub specie aeternitatis.* Genuine liberation follows only in the wake of a definitive detachment from the vicissitudes of the empirical ego. This imperative to de-individualize the ego is a characteristic feature found in the methodical practices of all manifestions of apophatic spirituality, which is sometimes referred to as the way of negation. This is the spirituality of the author of the Christian classic, *The Cloud of Unknowing.* It is a perspective familiar to all students of Plotinus, Ibn Arabi and Eckhart. *Cream of Liberation* proclaims: "This is the 'delight of knowledge' spoken of by the *Vedas.* Those who worship at the feet of Nârâyana are without blemish; those who, through the teacher of this pupil approach the stage in which doubt is finished and steadily go forward to perfection, will obtain spotless emancipation." This is the freedom of one who with "a detached outlook on the universe and its contents" lives in the "untainted awareness of the Self." This is the liberating ecstasy of the raindrop when it falls into the Sea.

In addition to addressing the meaning of freedom at its most profound level, these works also illuminate the question of what it means to be truly happy. *Lamp of Non-Dual Knowledge* states that most men, far removed from the knowledge of *Brahman,* live in a waking dream. Their daily lives are filled with transitory experiences of pleasure and pain which are no more real than clouds drifting across the sky. Just as in man's sleeping dreams one image follows after another, so in his waking dreams he passes through his life clinging to those experiences which make him happy, and trying to minimize all forms of suffering. The transitory nature of these experiences is illustrated by the fact that pleasure often turns to pain; for example, when a love affair goes wrong or when the wheel of fortune takes a downward turn. In waking dreams men feel happy to have a lucrative position, a loyal friend and a loving spouse. All of this, however, is subject to change. All that is born must die. The doctrine of

Vedânta teaches that the deep source of happiness can only be discovered in the eternity of *Brahman,* the ultimate Reality and ground of the universe. The nature of *Brahman* is *Sat-Chit-Ânanda* (Being-Knowledge-Bliss). This nature is pervasive throughout the universe, and it is only through specific methods of self-inquiry—such as Ramana Maharshi's question "Who am I"?—that a man seeking God may trace the manifestations of the phenomenal world back to the Reality of *Brahman.* This practice of *viveka* (discernment) between the Real and the unreal must be carried out under the supervision of a qualified Master. The message of Uddâlâka to Shvetaketu is that the Self, or *Âtman*—which is the spiritual substrate of the individual ego—is identical with *Brahman.* Man's greatest happiness is in the realization of this identity. In the words of Shankara: "The Self is Brahmâ, the Self is Vishnu, the Self is Indra, the Self is Shiva: the Self is all this universe. Nothing exists except the Self." *Lamp of Non-Dual Knowledge* is even more explicit and descriptive. In the chapter on realization we read the following words: "Just as at the end of a dream, the dreamer rising up as the waking experiencer says 'All along I was dreaming that I wandered in strange places, but I am only lying down on the bed,' or a madman cured of his madness remains pleased with himself, or a patient cured of his illness wonders at his past sufferings, or a poor man on becoming a king, forgets or laughs at his penurious state, or a man on becoming a celestial being enjoys a new bliss, or a devotee on uniting with the Lord of his devotion remains blissful, so also the *jîva* (individual soul) on emerging as *Brahman* wonders how all along being only *Brahman* he was moving about as a helpless being imagining a world, god and individuals, asks himself what became of all those fancies and how he now remaining all alone as Being-Knowledge-Bliss, free from any differentiation, internal or external, certainly experiences the supreme Bliss of *Brahman.*"

World Wisdom, with the kind cooperation of Sri Ramanasraman of Tiruvannamalai, is happy to bring these new editions of *Cream of Liberation* and *Lamp of Non-Dual Knowledge* to an expanded circle of readers. Among all of the explicitly formulated metaphysical doctrines found in the religions of the world, *Advaita Vedanta* is one of the most complete and clearly articulated. These two gems of *advaita*, taken from the crown of Indian wisdom, are distilled and near perfect presentations of the perennial Truth which lies at the heart of all religions. This underlying Religion has liberated countless souls and unfailingly guided *sâdhakas* (seekers) home since the *Vedic* period began some twelve hundred years before the birth of Christ.

Barry McDonald
World Wisdom
June 2002

The Lamp of
Non-Dual Knowledge

A Translation of
Advaita Bodha Deepika
by Sri Karapatra Swami

Translation into English by
Swami Sri Ramanananda Saraswathi

Foreword to the 1979 Edition

Originally, Shri Shankarâchârya and other great sages had written several works, like the commentary on the *Vedânta Sûtras*, and thus furnished the methods for those engaged in Self-enquiry to accomplish their purpose.

From those, Shri Karapatra Swâmi later condensed the salient points into Sanskrit verse in a work of twelve chapters, called *Shri Advaita Bodha Deepika*.

Still later, some great man seems to have translated this into Tamil prose. For some unknown reasons, only eight chapters of the same are found published. They are:

(1) *Adhyâropa* = Super-imposition.
(2) *Apavâda* = Its removal.
(3) *Sâdhana* = The means of accomplishment.
(4) *Shravana* = Hearing, reading, talking about God.
(5) *Manana* = Reflecting on shravana.
(6) *Vâsanâksaya* = Annihilation of latencies.
(7) *Sâkshâtkâra* = Direct Realization.
(8) *Manolaya* = Extinction of the mind.

In this work the author has explained how ignorance obscures the true nature of the Self which is non-dual only; how by its veiling aspect it covers It (the Self) with two effects—"that It does not exist" and "that It does not shine forth"; how by its other aspect, in the shape of the mind projecting individuals, *Îshvara* and the world, and presenting them as real, it thus gives rise to illusion; how one fully qualified is alone fit to obtain this knowledge; how a bare scholar of the *Shâstras* cannot be fit; how enquiry is the chief means for knowledge; how this enquiry consists in hearing of, reflecting upon and contemplation of The Truth, and *samâdhi*; how the indirect knowledge gained by hearing puts an end to the idea that "It does not exist" and the direct knowledge gained by reflection, which means enquiry into "Who I am" and seeking within, destroys the wrong notion that "It does not shine forth"; how the knowledge of "thou" in "That thou art" is identical with the knowledge of "That"; how by meditation, the different latencies perishing, which were the obstacle on the way, the mind, which is the limiting adjunct (upâdhi) of the individual, perishes too, and by the eventual unobstructed realization of *Brahman* (God) the seeker becomes free from the bondage of the three kinds of karma, which form the cycle of births and deaths; how in truth there is neither bondage nor release for the Self and in what way to extinguish the mind.

Thinking that this will be helpful to seekers of liberation Shri Swâmi Ramânananda Saraswathi (formerly Munagala Venkatara-miah), a devotee of Bhagavân has by the grace of Shri Ramana rendered into English the eight chapters of the work now available. The last four chapters, *Savikalpa Samâdhi, Nirvikalpa Samâdhi, Jîvan Mukti* and *Videha Mukti* not being found in Tamil, Telugu or Sanskrit Mss., could not be translated into English. Information on the missing chapters is earnestly sought and will be gratefully acknowledged by the publisher.

Our grateful thanks are due to H. H. Smt. Shânta Devi Mahârani of Baroda and H. H. the Mahârâja of Travancore for sending us the original Sanskrit Mss. of this work from the State Libraries for Maharshi's consultation and return.

This book is one of the few esteemed by Shri Maharshi and this translation was thoroughly revised in His Presence. So we are encouraged to present this small volume to the public with full confidence that the reader will benefit by it.

T. N. Venkataraman
President Board of Trustees
Sri Ramanasramam

Introduction

1. I salute the holy feet of the supreme Lord, the Refuge of all the universe, the one means to kill *samsâra* (the cycle of births and deaths), the eternal God Ganesha of elephant-face!

2. I meditate on the holy Master known as *chidambaran Brahman*, the very being of the non-dual supreme Self, Its very bliss and the foremost *yogi* among men by whose light-glance I, a fool, blinded by the massive darkness of beginningless ignorance, gained the precious jewel of *jñâna* (wisdom)!

3. I meditate on that holy Master, by contact with the dust of whose lotus-feet men are easily able to cross the shoreless ocean of *samsâra*, as if it were only a span.

4. & 5. To those who are fitted (by all) their sins having been burnt off by austerities (practiced) in several past births, their minds made pure, their intellects discriminating the real from the unreal, themselves indifferent to the pleasures of either this or the other world, their minds and senses under control, passions held down, actions given up as a worthless burden, faith firm and minds tranquil, eagerly seeking release from bondage, this work—*Shri Advaita Bodha Deepika*—is presented in twelve short chapters.

6. Many different works on *Advaita* have already appeared from Masters of yore, like Shri Shankarâchârya and Vidyâranya; yet as a fond parent loves to hear the broken words of the lisping child, so also good people with large hearts can read this work as well, imperfect as it may be.

Chapter I

Adhyâropa

On Superimposition

7. Greatly afflicted by the three kinds of distress *(tâpatraya)*, intensely seeking release from bondage so as to be free from this painful existence, a disciple distinguished by long practice of the four-fold *sâdhana,* approaches a worthy Master and prays:

8-12. "Lord, Master, ocean of mercy, I surrender to you! Pray save me!"

Master: Save you from what?

Disciple: From the fear of recurring births and deaths.

Master: Leave *samsâra* and fear not.

Disciple: Unable to cross this vast ocean of *samsâra,* I fear recurring births and deaths. So I have surrendered to you. It is for you to save me!

Master: What can I do for you?

Disciple: Save me. I have no other refuge. Just as water is the only thing to put out the flames when the hair of one's head is on fire, so also a sage such as you is the sole refuge of people like me, who are on fire from the three kinds of distress. You are free from the illusion of *samsâra,* calm in mind and sunk deep in the incomparable Bliss of *Brahman,* which is beginningless and endless. Certainly you can save this poor creature. Pray do!

Master: What is it to me if you suffer?

Disciple: Saints like you cannot bear to see others suffer, as a father his child. Motiveless is your love for all beings. You are the *guru* common to all, the only boat to carry us across this ocean of *samsâra.*

Master: Now, what makes you suffer?

Disciple: Bitten by the cruel serpent of painful *samsâra,* I am dazed and I suffer. Master, pray save me from this burning hell and kindly tell me how I can be free.

13-17. *M.:* Well said, my son! You are intelligent and well-disciplined. There is no need to prove your competence to be a disciple. Your words clearly show that you are fit. Now look here, my child!

In the supreme Self of Being-Knowledge-Bliss (*Sat-Chit-Ânanda*) who can be the transmigrating being? How can this *samsâra* be? What could have given rise to it? And how and whence can it arise itself? Being the non-dual Reality, how can you be deluded? With nothing separate in deep sleep, not having changed in any manner, and having slept soundly and peacefully, a fool on waking shouts out, "Alas, I am lost!" How can you, the changeless, formless, supreme, blissful Self shout forth, "I transmigrate. I am miserable!" and so on? Truly there is neither birth nor death; no one to be born or to die; nothing of the kind!

D.: What does exist then?

M.: There exists only the beginningless, endless, non-dual, never-bound, ever-free, pure, aware, single, Supreme, Bliss-Knowledge.

18. *D.:* If so, tell me how this mighty, massive delusion of *samsâra* veils me in dense darkness like a mass of clouds in the rainy season.

19-20. *M.:* What can be said of the power of this illusion (*Mâyâ*)? As a man mistakes a post for a man, so also you mistake the non-dual, perfect Self for an individual. Being deluded you are miserable. But how does this illusion arise? Like a dream in sleep, this false *samsâra* appears in the illusion of ignorance which is itself unreal. Hence your mistake.

21-24. *D.:* What is the ignorance?

M.: Listen. In the body appears a phantom, the "I"-conceit, to claim the body for itself, and it is called *jîva*. This *jîva* always has an outward bent, taking the world to be real and himself to be the doer and experiencer of pleasures and pains, desirous of this and that, undiscriminating, not once remembering his true nature, nor enquiring, "Who am I? What is this world?" but wandering in the *samsâra* without knowing himself. Such forgetfulness of the Self is ignorance.

25. D.: All the *shâstras* proclaim that this *samsâra* is the hand-iwork of *Mâyâ* but you say it is of ignorance. How are the two statements to be reconciled?

M.: This ignorance is called by different names, such as *Mâyâ, pradhâna, avyakta* (the unmanifest), *avidyâ*, Nature, Darkness and so on. Therefore samsâra is but the result of ignorance.

26. D.: How does this ignorance project the samsâra?

M.: Ignorance has two aspects: Veiling (*âvarana*) and projection (*vikshepa*). From these arises the *samsâra*. Veiling functions in two ways: in the one we say, "It is not," and in the other, "It does not shine forth".

27-28. D.: Please explain this.

M.: In a discourse between a Master and a student, although the sage teaches that there is only the non-dual Reality, the ignorant man thinks: "What can be non-dual Reality? No. It cannot be." As a result of beginningless veiling, though taught, the teaching is disregarded and the old ideas persist. Such indifference is the first aspect of veiling.

29-30. Next, with the help of sacred books and a gracious Master, he unaccountably but sincerely believes in the non-dual Real, yet he cannot probe deep and remains superficial, saying: "The Reality does not shine forth". Here is knowledge knowing that It does shine forth yet the illusion of ignorance persists. This illusion that It does not shine forth is the second aspect of veiling.

31-32. D.: What is projection?

M.: Though he is the unchanging, formless, supreme, blissful, non-dual Self, the man thinks of himself as the body with hands and legs, the doer and experiencer. He objectively sees this man and that man, this thing and that thing, and is deluded. This delusion of perceiving the external universe on the non-dual Reality enveloped by it, is projection. This is super-imposition (*adhyâropa*).

33. D.: What is superimposition?

M.: To mistake something which is, for something which is not—like a rope for a snake, a post for a thief, a mirage for water. The appearance of a false thing on a real, is superimposition.

34. D.: What is here the unreal superimposition on the real thing, the substratum?

M.: The non-dual Being-Knowledge-Bliss or the supreme *Brahman* is the Real. Just as the false name and form of snake is superimposed on a rope, so also on the non-dual Reality there is superimposed the category of sentient beings and insentient things. Thus the names and forms which appear as the universe, make up the superimposition. This is the unreal phenomenon.

D.: In the Reality which is non-dual, who is there to bring about this superimposition?

M.: It is *Mâyâ.*

D.: What is *Mâyâ?*

35. *M.:* It is the ignorance about the aforesaid *Brahman.*

D.: What is the ignorance?

M.: Though the Self is *Brahman*, there is not the knowledge of the Self (being *Brahman*). That which obstructs this knowledge of the Self is ignorance.

D.: How can this project the world?

M.: Just as ignorance of the substratum, namely the rope, projects the illusion of a snake, so ignorance of *Brahman* projects this world.

36. *M.:* It must be regarded an illusion because it is superimposed and does not exist either before (perception) or after (knowledge).

D.: How can it be said that it does not exist either before (perception) or after (knowledge)?

M.: In order to be created, it could not have been before creation (i.e., it comes into existence simultaneously with or after creation); in dissolution it cannot exist; now in the interval it simply appears like a magic-born city in mid-air. Inasmuch as it is not seen in deep sleep, shocks and *samâdhi*, it follows that even now it is only a superimposition and therefore an illusion.

37. *D.:* Before creation and in dissolution, if there is no world, what can exist then?

M.: There is only the basic Existence, non-fictitious, non-dual, undifferentiated, *ab extra* and *ab intra* (*ajâtîya, vijâtîya,* and *svagata bheda*), Being-Knowledge-Bliss, the unchanging Reality.

D.: How is it known?

M.: The *Vedas* say: "Before creation there was only pure

Being". *Yoga Vasishtha* also helps us to understand it.

D.: How?

38. *M.:* "In dissolution the whole universe is withdrawn leaving only the single Reality which stays motionless, beyond speech and thought, neither darkness nor light, yet perfect, namely, untellable, but not void," says the *Yoga Vasishtha*.

39. *D.:* In such non-duality how can the universe arise?

M.: Just as in the aforesaid rope-snake (example), the ignorance of the real substratum lies hidden in the rope, so also in the basic Reality there lies hidden ignorance, otherwise called *Mâyâ* or *avidyâ*. Later this gives rise to all these names and forms.

40-41. This *Mâyâ*, which is dependent on the unrelated Knowledge-Bliss-Reality, has the two aspects of veiling (*âvarana*) and projection (*vikshepa*); by the former it hides its own substratum from view; and by the latter the unmanifest *Mâyâ* is made manifest as mind. This then sports with its latencies, which leads to the projecting of this universe with all the names and forms.

42. *D.:* Has anyone else said this before?

M.: Yes, Vasishtha to Râma.

D.: How?

43-50. *M.:* The powers of *Brahman* are infinite. Among them, that power becomes manifest through which it shines forth.

D.: What are these different powers?

M.: Sentience in sentient beings; movement in air; solidity in earth; fluidity in water; heat in fire; void in the ether; the decaying tendency in the perishable; and many more are well-known. These qualities remained unmanifest and later manifested themselves. They must have been latent in the non-dual *Brahman* like the glorious colors of peacock feathers in the yolk of its egg or the spread out banyan tree in the tiny seed.

D.: If all powers lay latent in the single *Brahman* why did they not manifest simultaneously?

M.: Look how the seeds of trees, plants, herbs, creepers, etc. are all contained in the earth but only some of them sprout forth according to the soil, climate and season. So also the nature and extent of powers for manifestation are determined

11

by conditions. At the time *Brahman* (the substratum of all the powers of *Mâyâ*), joins the power of thinking, this power manifests as mind. Thus, *Mâyâ*, so long dormant, suddenly starts forth as mind from the supreme *Brahman*, the common source of all. Then this mind fashions all the universe. So says Vasishtha.

51. *D.:* What is the nature of this mind which forms the power of projection of *Mâyâ?*

M.: To recollect ideas or latencies is its nature. It has latencies as its content and appears in the witnessing consciousness in two modes:"I" and "this."

D.: What are these modes?

M.: They are the concept "I" and the concepts "this", "that", etc.

52. *D.:* How is this I-mode superimposed on the witnessing consciousness?

M.: Just as silver superimposed on nacre presents the nacre as silver, so also the I-mode on the basic witness presents it as "I" (i.e. the ego), as if the witness were not different from the ego but were the ego itself.

53. Just as a person possessed by a spirit is deluded and behaves as altogether a different person, so also the witness possessed by the I-mode forgets its true nature and presents itself as the ego.

54. *D.:* How can the unchanging witness mistake itself for the changing ego?

M.: Like a man in delirium feeling himself lifted in air, or a drunken man beside himself, or a madman raving incoherently, or a dreamer going on dream-journeys, or a man possessed behaving in strange ways, the witness, though himself untainted and unchanged, yet under the malicious influence of the phantom ego, appears changed as "I".

55. *D.:* Does the I-mode of mind present the witness altered as the ego, or itself appear modified as the ego in the witness?

56-57. *M.:* Now, this question cannot arise, for having no existence apart from the Self, it cannot manifest of itself. Therefore it must present the Self as if modified into the ego.

D.: Please explain it more.

M.: Just as the ignorance-factor in the rope cannot project itself as snake but must make the rope look like a snake; that in water unable to manifest itself, makes the water manifest as foam, bubbles and waves; that in fire, itself unable, makes the fire display itself as sparks; that in clay cannot present itself but presents the clay as a pot, so also the power in the witness cannot manifest itself but presents the witness as the ego.

58-60. *D.:* Master, how can it be said that through *Mâyâ* the Self is fragmented into individual egos? The Self is not related to anything else; it remains untainted and unchanged like ether. How can *Mâyâ* affect it? Is it not as absurd to speak of fragmentation of the Self as to say, "I saw a man taking hold of ether and moulding it into a man; or fashioning air into a cask?" I am now sunk in the ocean of *samsâra*. Please rescue me.

61. *M.:* *Mâyâ* is called *Mâyâ* because it can make the impossible possible. It is the power which brings into view what was not always there, like a magician making his audience see a celestial city in mid-air. If a man can do this, can *Mâyâ* not do that? There is nothing absurd in it.

62-66. *D.:* Please make it clear to me.

M.: Now consider the power of sleep to call forth dream visions. A man lying on a cot in a closed room falls asleep and in his dream wanders about taking the shapes of birds and beasts; the dreamer sleeping in his home, the dream presents him as walking in the streets of Benares or on the sands of Setu; although the sleeper is lying unchanged yet in his dream he flies up in the air, falls headlong into an abyss or cuts off his own hand and carries it in his hand. In the dream itself there is no question of consistency or otherwise. Whatever is seen in it appears to be appropriate and is not criticized. If simple sleep can make the impossible possible what wonder can there be in the almighty *Mâyâ* creating this indescribable universe? It is its very nature.

67-74. To illustrate it, I shall briefly tell you a story from the *Yoga Vasishtha*. There was once a king named Lavana, a jewel of the Ikshvâku line. One day when all were assembled in the court hall, a magician appeared before him. Quickly he approached the king, saluted and said: "Your Majesty, I shall show you a wonder, look!" At once he waved a flail of peacock feather before the king. The king was dazed, forgot himself and saw a great illusion like an extraordinary dream. He found a horse in front of him, mounted it and rode on it hunting in a forest. After hunting long, he was thirsty, could not find water and grew weary. Just then a low caste girl happened to come there with some coarse food in an earthen dish. Driven by hunger and thirst, he cast aside all restrictions of caste, and his own sense of dignity, and asked her for food and drink. She offered to oblige him only if she could be made his legitimate wife. Without hesitation he agreed, took the food given by her, and then went to her hamlet where they both lived as husband and wife and had two sons and one daughter.

All along the king remained on the throne. But in the short interval of an hour and a half, he had led another illusory life of wretchedness, extending over several years. In this way Vasishtha had related several long stories to Râma in order to impress on him the wonderful play of *Mâyâ* by which the impossible is easily made possible.

75-76. There is no illusion which is beyond the power of mind to spread, and no one not deluded by it. Its characteristic is to accomplish that which is impossible. Nothing can escape its power. Even the Self which is always unchanging and untainted, has been made to look changed and tainted.

D.: How can it be so?

M.: See how the sky which is impartite and untainted, looks blue. The supreme Self, too, though always pure, has been invested by it with the ego and is made to parade as *jîva,* just as *Lavana* the king lived as a low-caste wretch.

77. *D.:* If the supreme Self has, by joining the I-mode of the mind, become the illusory *jîva* he should appear as a single *jîva.* But there are many *jîva*s. How can the single Reality manifest as innumerable *jîva*s?

78-80. *M.:* As soon as the illusion of a single *jîva,* becomes operative in the pure supreme Self, it naturally begets other illusory *jîva*s in the pure ether of Knowledge. If a dog enters a room walled by mirrors, it first gives rise to one reflection in one mirror, which by a series of reflections becomes innumerable, and the dog finding itself surrounded by so many other dogs growls and shows fight. So it is with the Self of pure, non-dual ether of Consciousness. The illusion of one *jîva* is perforce associated with illusion of several *jîva*s.

81-83. Again, the habit of seeing the world as you, I, he, etc., forces the dreamer to see similar illusory entities in dreams also. Similarly, the accumulated habits of past births make the Self, which is only pure Knowledge-Ether see numberless illusory *jîva*s even now. What can be beyond the scope of *Mâyâ* which is itself inscrutable? Now this done, listen to how the bodies and the spheres were created.

84-85. Just as the supreme Self is presented as "I" by the I-mode of *Mâyâ*, so also It is presented by the "this"-mode as the universe with all its contents.

D.: How?

M.: The power of multiplicity is the "this"-mode whose nature is to be imagining "this" and "that". In the ether of Consciousness it recollects the millions of latencies, as "this" and "that". Being stirred up by these latencies, the *jîva* though itself the ether of Consciousness, now manifests as the individual body, etc., the external worlds and the diversities.

D.: How?

86-89. *M.:* First, mind appears in the impartite ether of Consciousness. Its movements form the aforesaid latencies which show forth in various illusory forms, such as, "here is the body with organs and limbs," "I am this body,"—"here is my father," "I am his son," "my age is such and such," "these are our relatives and friends,"—"this is our house," "I and you," "this and that," "good and bad," "pleasure and pain," "bondage and release," "castes, creeds and duties," "Gods, men and other creatures," "high, low and middling,"— "enjoyer and enjoyments," "many millions of spheres," and so on.

D.: How can the latencies themselves appear as this vast universe?

90. *M.:* A man, remaining unmoving and happy in deep sleep, when stirred up by the rising latencies, sees illusory dream-visions of creatures and worlds; they are nothing but the latencies in him. So in the waking state also, he is deluded by the latencies manifesting as these creatures and worlds.

91. *D.:* Now, Master, the dream is but the reproduction of mental impressions formed in the waking state and lying dormant before. They reproduce past experiences. Therefore dream-visions are rightly said to be only mental creations. Should the same be true of the waking world, this must be the reproduction of some past impressions. What are those impressions which give rise to these waking experiences?

92. *M.:* Just as the experiences of the waking state give rise to the dream-world, so also the experiences of past lives give rise to this world of the waking state, (which is) nonetheless illusory.

D.: If the present experience is the result of the preceding one, what gave rise to its preceding one?

M.: That was from its preceding one and so on.

D.: This can extend back to the time of creation. In dissolution all these impressions must have been resolved. What was left there to start the new creation?

M.: Just as your impressions gathered one day lie dormant in deep sleep and become manifest the following day, so also the impressions of the preceding cycle *(kalpa)* reappear in the succeeding one. Thus, these impressions of *Mâyâ* have no beginning, but appear over and over again.

93. *D.:* Master, what was experienced on previous days can now be remembered. Why do we not remember the experiences of past lives?

94-95. M.: This cannot be. See how the waking experiences repeat themselves in the dream but are apprehended in the same way as in the waking state, but differently. Why? Because sleep makes all the difference, inasmuch as it hides the original bearings and distorts them, so that the same experience repeated in the dream is differently set, often aberrant and wobbling. Similarly, the experiences of past lives have been affected by comas and deaths so that the present setting is different from the past ones and the same experience repeated in a different way cannot recall the past.

96. *D.:* Master, dream-visions being only mental creations are transient and are soon dismissed as unreal. So they are properly said to be illusory. On the contrary, the waking world is seen to be lasting and all evidence goes to show that it is real. How can

it be classified with dreams as being illusory?

97-98. *M.* : In the dream itself, the visions are experienced as proven and real; they are not at that time felt to be unreal. Similarly at the time of experience, this waking world also seems to be proven and real. But when you wake up to your true nature, this will also pass off as unreal.

D.: What then is the difference between the dream and waking states ?

99. M.: Both are only mental and illusory. There can be no doubt of this. Only, the waking world is a long, drawn-out illusion and the dream a short one. This is the only difference and nothing more.

100. *D.:* Should waking be only a dream, who is the dreamer here?

M.: All this universe is the dream-product of the non-dual, untainted, Knowledge-Bliss only.

D.: But a dream can happen only in sleep. Has the supreme Self gone to sleep in order to see this dream?

M.: Our sleep corresponds to Its ignorance which hides Its real nature from time immemorial. So It dreams the dream of this universe. Just as the dreamer is deluded into thinking himself the experiencer of his dreams, so also the unchanging Self is by illusion presented as a *jîva* experiencing this *samsâra.*

101. On seeing the dreamlike body, senses, etc., the *jîva* is deluded into the belief that he is the body, senses, etc.; with them he turns round and round through the waking, dream and deep sleep states. This forms his *samsâra.*

102-104. *D.:* What is *jâgrat* (the waking state)?

M.: It is the phenomenon of the I-mode along with all the other modes of mind and the related objects. Taking on I-ness in the gross body of the waking state, the individual goes by the name of *vishva,* the experiencer of the waking state.

D.: What is dream?

M.: After the senses are withdrawn from external activities the impressions formed by the mental modes of the waking state reproduce themselves as visions in dreams. The experiencer of this subtle state is known as the *taijasa.*

D. : What is deep sleep *(sushupti)* ?

M. : When all the mental modes lie dormant in causal ignorance, it is said to be deep sleep. Here the experiencer known as *prâjña* has the bliss of Self.

105. The *jîva* revolves in this merry-go-round owing to the operation of his past *karma* according as it bestows waking, dream or deep sleep experience. This is *samsâra*. In the same way the *jîva* is subject to births and deaths as a result of past *karma*.

106. Nevertheless, they are merely appearances of the deluded mind and not real. He (only) seems to be born and to die.

D.: How can birth and death be illusory?

M.: Listen carefully to what I say.

107-109. Just as when the *jîva* is overcome by sleep, the bearings of the waking state give place to new ones of dream in order to reproduce past experiences, or there is a total loss of all external things and mental activities, so also when he is overpowered by coma before death, the present bearings are lost and the mind lies dormant. This is death. When the mind resumes the reproduction of past experiences in new settings, the phenomenon is called birth. The process of birth starts with the man's imagining: "Here is my mother; I lie in her womb; my body has those limbs". Then he imagines himself born into the world, and later says: "This is my father; I am his son; my age is such and such; these are my relatives and friends; this fine house is mine," and so on. This series of new illusions begins with the loss of former illusions in the coma before death, and depends upon the results of past actions.

110-113. The *jîva* overpowered by the unreal coma before death has different illusions according to his different past actions. After death, he believes: "Here is heaven; it is very lovely; I am in it; I am now a wonderful celestial being; so many charming celestial damsels are at my service; I have nectar for drink," or, "Here is the region of death; here is the god of death; these are the messengers of Death; Oh! they are so cruel—they pitch me into hell!" or, "Here is the region of the *pitris;* or of Brahmâ; or of Vishnu; or of Shiva," and so on. Thus, according to their nature, the latencies of past *karma* present themselves before the Self, who remains always the unchanging ether of Consciousness, as illusions of birth, death, passage to heaven, hell or other regions. They are only delusions of the mind and not real.

114. In the Self of the ether of Consciousness there is the phenomenon of the universe, like a celestial city seen in mid-air. It is fancied to be real but is not indeed so. Names and forms make it up and it is nothing more.

115. *D.:* Master, not only I, but all others, directly experience this world of sentient beings and insentient things and take it as proven and real. How is it said to be unreal?

116. *M.:* The world, with all its contents, is only superimposed upon the ether of Consciousness.

D.: By what is it superimposed?

M.: By ignorance of the Self.

D.: How is it superimposed?

M.: As a painting of sentient beings and insentient things presents a scene upon a background.

117. *D.:* Whereas the scriptures declare that all this universe was created by the will of *Îshvara*, you say it is by one's own ignorance. How can these two statements be reconciled?

118. *M.:* There is no contradiction. What the scriptures say— that *Îshvara*, by means of *Mâyâ*, created the five elements and mixed them up in diverse ways to make the diversities of the universe—is all false.

D.: How can the scriptures say what is false?

M.: They are guides to the ignorant and do not mean what they appear to on the surface.

D.: How is that?

M.: Man, having forgotten his true nature of being the all-perfect ether of Consciousness, is deluded by ignorance into identifying himself with a body, etc., and regarding himself as an insignificant individual of mean capacity. If to him it is told that he is the creator of the whole universe, he will flout the idea and refuse to be guided. So, coming down to his level, the scriptures posit an *Îshvara* as the Creator of the universe. But it is not the truth. However, the scriptures reveal the truth to the competent seeker. You are now mistaking the nursery tale for metaphysical truth. In this connection you may remember the child's tale in *Yoga Vasishtha*.

119-134. *D.:* What is it?

M.: It is a fine story to illustrate the emptiness of this universe. On hearing it the false notions of the world being real and its creation by *Îshvara*, will all disappear. Briefly put, the story runs as follows: A child asked its nurse to tell an interesting story. Accordingly she told the following:

Nurse: Once upon a time a most powerful king whose mother was barren, ruled over all the three worlds. His word was law to all the kings in these worlds. The barren mother's son had extraordinary powers of illusion to make, foster and unmake worlds. At his will he could take on any one of the three bodies: white, yellow or black. When he took on the yellow body, he had an urge and would, like a magician, create a city.

Child: Where is that city?

N.: It hangs in mid-air.

C.: What is it called?

N.: Absolute Unreality.

C.: How is it built up?

N.: It has fourteen royal roads, each divided into three sections in which there are respectively many pleasure gardens, huge mansions and seven luxurious tanks—adorned with strings of pearls. Two lamps—one warm and the other cool—always light the city. In it the barren mother's son built many fine houses, some on high, some in the middle and others on low ground. Each of them has a black velvety top, nine gateways, several windows to let in the breeze, five lamps, three white pillars, and walls plastered nicely. By his magic he created fearsome phantoms, one to guard each house. As a bird enters its nest, he enters any of these houses at his will and sports at his pleasure.

135-140. With his black body, he protects these homes through the phantom guards. With his white body he instantaneously reduces them to ashes. This barren woman's son, who like a fool repeatedly produces, protects and destroys the city at his whim, was once tired after his work, refreshed himself bathing in the quaffing waters of mirage and proudly wore flowers gathered from the sky. I have seen him; he will soon come here to present you with four strings of gems made from the lustre of broken fragments of glass and anklets of nacre-silver.

The child believed the tale and was pleased. So it is with the fool who takes this world to be real.

141-148. *D.:* How, does this story illustrate the point?

M.: The child of the legend is the ignorant man of the world; the wet-nurse is the scripture which speaks of the creation by *Îshvara*; the barren mother's son is the *Îshvara* born of *Mâyâ*; his three bodies are the three qualities of *Mâyâ*; his assumption of the bodies is the aspect of Brahmâ, Vishnu or Rudra. In the yellow body Brahmâ who is the thread running through the whole universe, creates it in the ether of Consciousness, which corresponds to mid-air in the fable; its name is Absolute Unreality; the fourteen royal roads are the fourteen worlds; the pleasure gardens are the forests; the mansions are the mountain ranges; the two lamps are the sun and the moon; and the luxurious tanks adorned with strings of pearls are the oceans into which so many rivers flow.

149-155. The houses built on the high, middle and low ground, are the bodies of the celestials, men and animals; the three white pillars are the skeleton of bones; and the plaster on the walls is the skin; the black top is the head with hair on it; the nine gateways are the nine passages in the body; the five lamps are the five senses; and the phantom watchman is the ego.

Now *Îshvara* the king, who is the son of the barren mother *Mâyâ*, having built the houses of the bodies, enters into them at will as the *jîvas*, sports in the company of the phantom egos and moves about aimlessly.

156-160. With the black body he functions as Vishnu, otherwise known as *Virât*, and sustains the universe. With the white body as Rudra, the Destroyer, the In-dweller in all, he withdraws the whole universe into himself. This is his sport and he is pleased with it. This pleasure is said to be the king's refreshing himself in the waters of mirage. His pride is of his sovereignty. The blossoms from the sky are the attributes of omniscience and omnipotence. The anklets are heaven and hell; the four strings of glass-lustre are the four stages of *mukti*: *sâlôkya, samîpya, sarupya* and *sayujya*, meaning equality in rank, condition or power and final identity. The king's expected arrival to present the gifts is the image-worship which fulfills the prayers of the devotees.

In this manner the ignorant student of the scriptures is deluded by his ignorance into believing the world to be real.

161. *D.:* Should heaven and hell and the four stages of beatitude *(mukti)* be all false, why should a part of the scriptures prescribe methods of gaining heaven or beatitude?

162-164. *M.:* On seeing her child suffer from pain in the stomach, a fond mother desirous of administering pepper to the child, but aware of the child's dislike of pepper and love of honey, gently coaxes the child with a smear of honey before forcing the pepper into its mouth. In the same way the scriptures, in their mercy, seeing the ignorant student suffer in the world, desirous of making him realize the truth, but knowing his love for the world and dislike of the non-dual Reality which is subtle and hard to understand, gently coax him with the sweet pleasures of heaven, etc., before laying bare the non-dual Reality.

165. *D.:* How can the ideas of heaven, etc., lead him on to the non-dual Reality?

M.: By right actions, heaven is gained; by austerities and devotion to *Vishnu,* the four stages of beatitude. On knowing it a man practices what he likes among these. By repeated practices in several rebirths his mind becomes pure and turns away from sense-enjoyments to receive the highest teaching of the non-dual Reality.

166. *D.:* Master, admitting heaven, hell, etc., to be false, how can *Îshvara* so often mentioned by the scriptures, be also declared unreal?

167. *M.:* Well, passages dealing with *Îshvara* in all His glory, are succeeded by others which say that *Îshvara* is the product of *Mâyâ,* and the *jîva* of ignorance *(avidyâ).*

D.: Why do the scriptures contradict themselves with passages of different import?

M.: Their aim is to make the student purify his mind by his own efforts such as good actions, austerities and devotion. To coax him, these are said to yield him pleasures. Being themselves insentient, these cannot of their own accord yield fruits. So an all-powerful *Îshvara* is said to dispense the fruits of actions. That is how an *Îshvara* appears on the scene. Later the scriptures say that the *jîva, Îshvara* and the *jagat* (world) are all equally false.

168. *Îshvara*, the product of illusion, is no more real than the dream-subject, the product of sleep. He is in the same category as the *jîva*, the product of ignorance, or of the dream-subject, the product of sleep.

169-174. *D.:* The scriptures say that *Îshvara* is the product of *Mâyâ*. How can we say that He is of ignorance?

M.: The ignorance of the Self may function singly or totally as we speak of single trees or a whole forest. The total ignorance of all the universe is called *Mâyâ*. Its product *Îshvara* functions as *Virât* in the universal waking state; as *Hiranyagarbha* in the universal dream state, and as the Indweller in the universal deep sleep. He is omniscient and omnipotent. Beginning with the will to create and ending with the entry into all creatures, this is His *samsâra*. The individual ignorance is said to be simply ignorance. Its product, the *jîva*, functions respectively as *vishva*, *taijasa* and *prâjña* in the individual waking, dream and deep sleep states. His knowledge and capacity are limited. He is said to be doer and enjoyer. His *samsâra* consists of all that lies between the present wakeful activities and final liberation. In this way the scriptures have made it clear that *Îshvara*, the *jîva* and the *jagat* are all illusory.

175-179. *D.:* Now, Master, just as the ignorance of the rope can give rise to the illusion only of a snake, so one's ignorance may spread the illusion of oneself being a *jîva*. But how can it be extended to create the illusions of *Îshvara* and *jagat* as well?

M.: Ignorance has no parts; it acts as a whole and produces all the three illusions at the same time. The *jîva* manifesting in the waking and dream states, *Îshvara* and *jagat* also manifest. As the *jîva* is resolved, the others are also resolved. This is proved by our experience of the waking and dream manifestations, and their disappearance in deep sleep, swoons, death and *samâdhi*.

Moreover, simultaneous with the final annihilation of *jîva*-hood by knowledge, the others also are finally annihilated along with it. The sages whose ignorance has completely been lost with all its attendant illusions and who are aware only as the Self, directly experience the non-dual Reality. Hence it is clear that the ignorance of the Self is the root-cause of all the three illusions—*jîva, jagat* and *Îshvara.*

180. *D.:* Master, should *Îshvara* be the illusion of ignorance, He must manifest as such. Instead, He appears as the origin of the universe and our Creator. It does not look reasonable to say that *Îshvara* and the *jagat* are both illusory products. Instead of appearing as our creation, He appears as our Creator. Is it not contradictory?

181-183. *M.:* No. In dreams the dreamer sees his father who was long ago dead. Though the father is created by himself as an illusion of dream, the dreamer feels that the other is the father and himself the son, and that he has inherited the father's property which again is his own creation. Now look how the dreamer creates individuals and things, relates himself to them and thinks that they were before, and he came after. So also with the *Îshvara*, the *jagat* and the *jîva.* This is only the trick of *Mâyâ* who can make the impossible possible.

D.: How is *Mâyâ* so powerful?

M.: No wonder. See how an ordinary magician can make a whole audience see a celestial city in mid-air or how you can yourself create a wonderful world of your own in your dreams. If such is possible for individuals of mean powers, how can the other not be possible for *Mâyâ* which is the universal material cause? To conclude: all these including *Îshvara, jîva* and *jagat* are illusory appearances resulting from one's ignorance and superimposed on the one Reality, the Self.

This leads us to consider the ways of removing the superimposition.

Chapter II

Apavâda

The Removal of Superimposition

1. *D.:* Master, ignorance is said to have no beginning; it follows that it will have no end. How can the beginningless ignorance be dispelled? Being the ocean of mercy can you please tell me this.

2. *M.:* Yes, my child; you are intelligent and can understand subtle things. You have said right. Truly, ignorance has no beginning, but it has an end. It is said that the rise of knowledge is the end of ignorance. Just as the sunrise dispels the darkness of night so also the light of knowledge dispels the darkness of ignorance.

3-4. To avoid confusion, everything in the world can be considered by analyzing its individual characteristics under the categories: cause, nature, effect, limit and fruit. But the transcendental Reality, being non-dual, is beyond all these whereas all else, from *Mâyâ* onwards, being wrongly seen on It, are subject to the above analysis.

5. Of these, *Mâyâ* has no antecedent cause because it is not the product of anything preceding it, but remains in *Brahman*, self-evident and without beginning. Before creation, there could be no cause for its manifestation, yet it manifests and it must be by itself.

6. *D.:* Is there any authority for this statement?

M.: Yes, Vasishtha's words. He says: Just as bubbles spontaneously arise in water so also the power to manifest names and forms rose up from the all-powerful and perfect transcendental Self.

7-9. *D.:* *Mâyâ* cannot but have a cause. Just as clay cannot become a pot without the agency of a potter so also the power all along remaining unmanifest in *Brahman* can manifest only with *Îshvara*'s will.

M.: In dissolution there remains only the non-dual *Brahman* and no *Îshvara.* Clearly there cannot be His will. When it is said that in dissolution all are withdrawn from manifestation and remain unmanifest, it means that the *jîvas,* all the universe, and *Îshvara,* have all become unmanifest. The unmanifest *Îshvara* cannot exercise His will. What happens is this: just as the dormant power of sleep displays itself as dream, so the dormant power of *Mâyâ* displays itself as this plurality, consisting of *Îshvara,* His will, the universe and the *jîvas. Îshvara* is thus the product of *Mâyâ* and He cannot be the origin of His origin. *Mâyâ* therefore has no antecedent cause. In dissolution there remains only pure Being devoid of will, and admitting of no change. In creation, *Mâyâ,* hitherto remaining unmanifest in this pure Being, shines forth as the mind. By the play of mind, plurality appears as *Îshvara,* the worlds and the *jîvas,* like magic. *Mâyâ* manifest is creation, and *Mâyâ* unmanifest is dissolution. Thus, of its own accord, *Mâyâ* appears or withdraws itself and has thus no beginning. Therefore we say there was no antecedent cause for it.

10-11. *D.:* What is its "nature"?

M.: It is inexpressible. Because its existence is later invalidated, it is not real; because it is factually experienced, it is not unreal; nor can it be a mixture of the two opposites, the real and the unreal. Therefore the wise say that it is indescribable *(anirvachaniya).*

D.: Now what is real and what is unreal?

M.: That which is the substratum of *Mâyâ,* pure Being or *Brahman,* admitting of no duality, is real. The illusory phenomenon, consisting of names and forms, and called the universe is unreal.

D.: What can *Mâyâ* be said to be?

M.: Neither of the two. It is different from the real substratum and also from the unreal phenomenon.

D.: Please explain this.

12-17. M.: Say there is fire; it is the substratum. The sparks fly off from it. They are the modifications of fire. The sparks are not seen in the fire itself, but come out of it. An observation of this phenomenon makes us infer a -power inherent in fire which produces the sparks.

Clay is the substratum; a hollow sphere with a neck and open mouth is made out of it, and is called a pot. This fact makes us infer a power which is neither clay nor pot but different from both.

Water is the substratum; bubbles are its effects. A power different from both is inferred.

A snake-egg is the substratum and a young snake is the product; a power different from the egg and the young snake is inferred.

A seed is the substratum and the sprout, its product; a power different from the seed and the sprout is inferred.

The changing *jîva* of deep sleep is the substratum and dream is the effect; a power different from the *jîva* and the dream is inferred after waking up from sleep.

In the same way the power lying latent in *Brahman* produces the illusion of the *jagat*. The substratum of this power is *Brahman* and the *jagat* is its effect. This power cannot be either of them, but must be different from both. It cannot be defined. However, it exists. But it remains inscrutable. Therefore we say the "nature" of *Mâyâ* is indescribable.

18-20. D.: What is the "effect" of *Mâyâ?*

M.: It consists in presenting the illusion of the *jîva, Îshvara* and *jagat* on the non-dual substratum of *Brahman*, by virtue of its veiling and projecting powers.

D.: How?

M.: As soon as the power lying dormant shows forth as mind, the latencies of the mind sprout forth and grow up like trees which together form the universe. The mind sports with its latencies; they rise up as thoughts and materialize as this universe, which is thus only a dream vision. The *jîva*s and *Îshvara* being its contents, are as illusory as this day-dream.

D.: Please explain their illusory character.

M.: The world is an object and seen as the result of the sport of mind. The *jîva*s and *Îshvara* are contained in it. Parts can be only as real as the whole. Suppose the universe is painted in colors on a wall. The *jîva*s and *Îshvara* will be figures in the painting. The figures can be only as real as the painting itself.

27

21-24. Here the universe is itself a product of the mind and *Îshvara* and the *jîvas* form parts of the same product. Therefore, they must be only mental projections and nothing more. This is clear from the *shruti* which says that *Mâyâ* gave rise to the illusions of *Îshvara* and the *jîvas*, and from the Vasishtha *smriti* where Vasishtha says that, as if by magic, the latencies dance about in the mind as, he, I, you, this, that, my son, property, etc.

25-27. *D.:* Where does this *smriti* speak of *Îshvara*, *jîva* and *jagat?*

M.: In this statement *sohamidam*, i.e., "He, I, this," "He" means the unseen *Îshvara;* "I" means the *jîva* parading as the ego, the doer, etc.; and "this" means all the objective universe. From scriptures, reasoning and experience *(shrutyuktyânubhâva)* it is clear that the *jîva, Îshvara* and *jagat* are only mental projections.

28-29. *D.:* How do reasoning and experience support this view?

M.: With the rise of mind in waking and dream, the latencies come into play, and the *jîvas, Îshvara* and *jagat* appear. With the subsidence of the latencies in deep sleep, swoon etc., they all disappear. This is within the experience of everyone.

Again when all the latencies are rooted out by knowledge, the *jîvas, Îshvara* and the *jagat* disappear once for all. This is within the experience of perfectly clear-sighted great sages established in the non-dual Reality, beyond the *jîvas Îshvara* and *jagat.* Therefore we say that these are all projections of the mind. Thus is explained the "effect" of *Mâyâ.*

30-32. *D.:* What is the "limit" of *Mâyâ?*

M.: It is the knowledge resulting from an enquiry into the sense of the *Mahâvâkyas.* Because *Mâyâ* is ignorance, and ignorance subsists on non-enquiry. When non-enquiry gives place to enquiry, right knowledge results and puts an end to ignorance.

Now listen. Ailments in the body are the results of past *karma;* they subsist on wrong diet and increase with its continuation. Or, the ignorance of rope, so long as it is not enquired into, projects a snake into view and other hallucinations follow in its wake. In the same manner although *Mâyâ* is self-evident, beginningless and spontaneous, yet it subsists in the absence of enquiry into the nature of the Self, manifests the universe etc., and grows more massive.

33-35. With the rise of enquiry, *Mâyâ*, hitherto grown strong by its absence, loses its nourishment and gradually withers away along with its effects, namely the *jagat* etc. Just as in the absence of enquiry the ignorance factor of rope made it look a snake but suddenly disappeared with the rise of enquiry, so also *Mâyâ* flourishes in ignorance and disappears with the rise of enquiry. Just as the rope-snake and the power which produces this illusion persist before enquiry, but after enquiry end in simple rope, so also *Mâyâ* and its effect, the *jagat,* persist before enquiry, but end in pure *Brahman* afterwards.

36-38. *D.:* How can a single thing appear in two different ways?

M.: Brahman, the non-dual pure Being, presents itself as the *jagat* before enquiry, and shows Itself in Its true form after enquiry.

See how before proper consideration clay appears a pot and afterwards as clay only; or gold appears as ornaments and then is found to be only gold. Similarly with *Brahman* too; after enquiry *Brahman* is realized to be unitary, non-dual, impartite, and unchanged in the past, present or future. In it there is nothing like *Mâyâ*, or its effect, such as the *jagat.* This realization is known as the supreme Knowledge and the limit of ignorance. Thus is described the "limit" of *Mâyâ*.

39. *D.:* What is the 'fruit' of *Mâyâ?*

M.: That it fruitlessly vanishes into nothing, is its fruit. A hare's horn is mere sound having no significance. So it is with *Mâyâ*: mere sound without any meaning. Realized sages have found it so.

40-43. *D.:* Then why do not all agree on this point?

M.: The ignorant believe it to be real. Those who are thoughtful will say it is indescribable. Realized sages say that it is non-existent like the hare's horn. It thus appears in these three ways. People will speak of it from their own points of view.

D.: Why do the ignorant consider it real?

M.: Even when a lie is told to frighten a child, that there is a spirit, the child believes it to be true. Similarly the ignorant are dazed by *Mâyâ* and believe it to be real. Those who enquire into the nature of the real *Brahman* and of the unreal *jagat* in the light of the scriptures, finding *Mâyâ* different from either and, unable to determine its nature, say it is indescribable. But sages who have attained Supreme Knowledge through enquiry say, "Like a mother burnt down to ashes by her daughter, *Mâyâ* reduced to ashes by knowledge is non-existent at any time."

44.46. *D.:* How can *Mâyâ* be compared to a mother burnt down to ashes by her daughter?

M.: In the process of enquiry, *Mâyâ* becomes more and more transparent and turns into Knowledge. Knowledge is thus born of *Mâyâ*, and is therefore said to be the daughter of *Mâyâ*. *Mâyâ*, so long flourishing on non-enquiry, comes to its last days on enquiry. Just as a crab brings forth its young only to die itself, so also in the last days of enquiry, *Mâyâ* brings forth knowledge for its own undoing. Immediately, the daughter knowledge, burns her down to ashes.

D.: How can the progeny kill the parent?

M.: In a bamboo forest, the bamboos move in the wind, rub against one another and produce fire which burns down the parent trees. So also, knowledge born of *Mâyâ* burns *Mâyâ* to ashes. *Mâyâ* remains only in name like a hare's horn. Therefore the sages declare it non-existent. Moreover, the very name implies its unreality. The names are *avidyâ* and *Mâyâ*. Of these the former means "ignorance, or that which is not"; again, "*Mâyâ* is that which is not". Therefore it is simple negation. Thus, that it fruitlessly vanishes into nothing is its "fruit".

47-49. *D.:* Master, *Mâyâ* turns into knowledge. Therefore it cannot be said to vanish fruitlessly as nothing.

M.: Only if the knowledge, the modified *Mâyâ*, be real, can *Mâyâ* be said to be real. But this knowledge is itself false. Therefore *Mâyâ* is false.

D.: How is knowledge said to be false?

M.: The fire from the friction of the trees burns them down and then dies out; the clearing-nut carries down the impurities of water and itself settles down with them. Similarly, this knowledge destroys ignorance and itself perishes. Since it is also finally resolved, the "fruit" of *Mâyâ* can be only unreal.

50-52. *D.:* Should knowledge also vanish in the end, how can *samsâra*, the effect of ignorance, be eradicated?

M.: Samsâra, the effect of ignorance, is unreal like knowledge. One unreality can be undone by another unreality.

D.: How can it be done?

M.: A dream-subject's hunger is satisfied by dream-food. The one is as unreal as the other and yet serves the purpose. Similarly, though Knowledge is unreal, yet it serves the purpose. Bondage and release are only false ideas of ignorance. As the appearance and disappearance of rope-snake are equally false, so also are bondage and release in *Brahman*.

54-55. To conclude: the supreme Truth is only the non-dual *Brahman*. All else is false and does not exist at any time. The *shrutis* support it saying: "Nothing is created or destroyed; there is no bondage or deliverance; no one is bound or desirous of release; there is no aspirant, no practitioner and no one liberated. This is the supreme Truth." Removal of superimposition thus consists in the knowledge of non-dual Reality, pure Being, beyond *Mâyâ* and its effects. Its realization is liberation while alive in the body (*jîvan-mukti*).

56. Only a careful student of this chapter can be desirous of knowing the process of enquiry into the Self as a means of undoing the superimposition of ignorance. The seeker fit for such enquiry must possess the fourfold qualities which will be dealt with in the next chapter. Then thc method of enquiry will be dealt with.

A competent seeker must carefully study these two chapters before proceeding further.

Chapter III

Sâdhanâ

The Means of Accomplishment

1. To the question, "How can there be *samsâra* for the supreme Self of Being-Knowledge-Bliss ?", the sages answer: "When unmanifest, the power of the Self is called *Mâyâ*, and when manifest, the same is mind. This mode of *Mâyâ*, the inscrutable mind, is the sprout of *samsâra* for the self".

D.: Who has said that mind is indescribable?

2-3. *M.:* Vasishtha has said to Râma. In the non-dual Consciousness the *bhâva* which, different from knowledge that is real and different from insentience that is unreal, tending to create, projects the latencies as this thing and that thing, mixes together the conscious and unconscious, and makes them appear under the categories, "the sentient" and "the insentient", itself of the nature of both the sentient and insentient. Always vacillating and changeful is mind. Therefore it is indescribable.

4. Though itself unchanging, the Supreme Self associated with the wrongly superimposed mind, appears to be changeful.

D.: How is that?

M.: Just as a *brahmin* who is drunk, behaves strangely when in the power of liquors, so too the Self though unchanged by nature, associated now with mind, appears changed as the *jîva* wallowing in this *samsâra*. Hence, the Self's *samsâra* is not other than mind. The *shrutis* say so.

5. Mind being the *samsâra*, must be investigated. Associated with the mind, which according to its modes assumes the shapes of objects, the man seems to undergo the same changes.

This eternal secret is disclosed in the *Maitrâyinîya Upanishad.* This is also confirmed by our experience and by positive and negative induction.

6-7. *D.:* How is it confirmed by our experience?

M.: When in deep sleep the mind lies quiescent, the Self remains without change and without *samsâra*. When in dream and waking, the mind manifests, and the Self seems changed and caught up in the *samsâra*. Everyone knows it by experience. It is evident from *shruti*, *smriti*, logic and experience that this *samsâra* is nothing but mind itself. How can any one dispute this point which is so obvious?

8-9. *D.:* How does association with mind entangle the Self in *samsâra*?

M.: Mind, whose nature is always to be thinking of this and that, functions in the two modes:the I-mode and "this"-mode, as already mentioned in Chapter I on superimposition. Of these two, the I-mode has always the single concept "I", whereas the "this"-mode varies according to the quality operating at the time, *sattva*, or *rajas*, or *tamas*, i.e., clearness, or activity or dullness.

D.: Who has said so before?

10-11. *M.:* Shri Vidyâranyaswâmi has said that the mind has these qualities, *sattva*, *rajas* and *tamas* and changes accordingly. In *sattva*, dispassion, peace, beneficence, etc., manifest; in *rajas*, desire, anger, greed, fear, efforts, etc., manifest; in *tamas*, sloth, confusion, dullness, etc.

12-14. Though unchanged pure Knowledge by nature, the Supreme Self, when associated with the mind changing according to the operative qualities, becomes identified with it.

D.: How can that be?

M.: You see how water is of itself cold and tasteless. Yet by association, it can be hot, sweet, bitter, sour, etc. Similarly the Self, by nature Being-Knowledge-Bliss, when associated with the I-mode, appears as the ego. Just as cold water in union with heat becomes hot, so also the blissful Self in union with the I-mode becomes the misery-laden ego. Just as water, originally tasteless, becomes sweet, bitter or sour according to its associations, so also the Self of pure Knowledge appears dispassionate, peaceful, beneficent; or passionate, angry, greedy; or dull and indolent, according to the quality of the "this"-mode at the moment.

15. The *shruti* says that the Self associated with *prâna*, etc., appears respectively as *prâna*, mind, intellect, the earth and the other elements, desire, anger, etc., dispassion, etc.

16. Accordingly, associated with the mind, the Self seems changed to *jîva*, sunk in the misery of endless *samsâra*, being deluded by innumerable illusions like I, you, it, mine, yours, etc.

17. *D.:* Now that *samsâra* has fallen to the lot of the Self, how can it be gotten rid of?

M.: With complete stillness of mind, *samsâra* will disappear root and branch. Otherwise there will be no end to *samsâra*, even in millions of aeons *(kalpakôtikâla)*.

18. *D.:* Cannot *samsâra* be gotten rid of by means other than making the mind still?

M.: Absolutely by no other means; neither the *Vedas* nor the *shâstras*, nor austerities, nor *karma*, nor vows, nor gifts, nor recital of scriptures or mystic formulae *(mantras)*, nor worship, nor anything else, can undo the *samsâra*. Only stillness of mind can accomplish the end and nothing else.

19. *D.:* The scriptures declare that only Knowledge can do it. How then can you say that stillness of the mind puts an end to *samsâra*?

M.: What is variously described as knowledge, liberation, etc., in the scriptures, is but stillness of mind.

D.: Has any one said so before?

20-27. *M.:* Vasishtha has said : When by practice, the mind stands still, all illusions of *samsâra* disappear, root and branch. Just as when the ocean of milk was churned for its nectar, it was all rough, but became still and clear after the churn (namely, Mt. Mandâra) was taken out, so also the mind becoming still, the *samsâra* falls to eternal rest.

D.: How can the mind be brought to stillness?

M.: By dispassion, abandoning all that is dear to oneself, one can by one's efforts accomplish the task with ease. Without this peace of mind, liberation is impossible. Only when the whole objective world is wiped out clean by a mind disillusioned, as a consequence of discerning knowledge that all that is not Brahman is objective and unreal, the Supreme Bliss will result. Otherwise in the absence of peace of mind, however much an ignorant man may struggle and creep on in the deep abyss of the *shâstras,* he cannot gain liberation.

Only that mind which by practice of *yoga,* having lost all its latencies, has become pure and still like a lamp in a dome well-protected from breeze, is said to be dead. This death of mind is the highest fulfillment. The final conclusion of all the *Vedas* is that liberation is nothing but mind stilled.

For liberation nothing can avail: not wealth, relatives, friends, *karma* consisting of movements of the limbs, pilgrimage to sacred places, baths in sacred waters, life in celestial regions, austerities however severe, or anything but a still mind. In similar strain many sacred books teach that liberation consists in doing away with the mind. In several passages in the *Yoga* Vasishtha, the same idea is repeated, that the bliss of liberation can be reached only by wiping out the mind, which is the root-cause of *samsâra,* and thus of all misery.

28. In this way to kill the mind by a knowledge of the sacred teaching, reasoning and one's own experience, is to undo the *samsâra.* How else can the miserable round of births and deaths be brought to a standstill ? And how can freedom result from it? Never. Unless the dreamer awakes, the dream does not come to an end, nor does the fright of being face-to-face with a tiger in the dream. Similarly, unless the mind is disillusioned, the agony of *samsâra* will not cease. Only the mind must be made still. This is the fulfillment of life.

29-30. *D.:* How can the mind be made still?

M.: Only by *Sânkhya. Sânkhya* is the process of enquiry coupled with knowledge. The realized sages declare that the mind has its root in non-enquiry and perishes by an informed enquiry.

D.: Please explain this process.

M.: This consists of *shravana, manana, nididhyâsana* and *samâdhi,* i.e., hearing, reasoning, meditation and blissful Peace, as mentioned in the scriptures. Only this can make the mind still.

31-32. There is also an alternative. It is said to be *yoga.*

D.: What is *yoga?*

M.: Meditation on pure Being free from qualities.

D.: Where is this alternative mentioned and how?

M.: In the *Gîtâ*, Bhagavân Shri Krishna has said: What is gained by *Sânkhya* can also be gained by *yoga*. Only he who knows that the result of the two processes is the same, can be called a realized sage.

33-34. *D.:* How can the two results be identical?

M.: The final "limit" is the same for both because both of them end in stillness of mind. This is *samâdhi* of blissful Peace. The "fruit" of *samâdhi* is supreme Knowledge; this remains the same by whichever process gained.

D.: If the "fruit" is the same for both, the final purpose can be served by only one of them. Why should two processes be mentioned instead of only one?

M.: In the world, seekers of truth are of different grades of development. Out of consideration for them, Shri Bhagavân has mentioned these two in order to offer a choice.

35. *D.:* Who is fit for the path of enquiry (*Sânkhya*)?

M.: Only a fully qualified seeker is fit, for he can succeed in it and not others.

36-37. *D.:* What are the *sâdhanâs* or requisites for this process?

M.: The knowers say that the *sâdhanâs* consist of an ability to discern the real from the unreal, no desire for pleasures here or hereafter, cessation of activities *(karma)* and a keen desire to be liberated. One not qualified with all these four qualities, however hard he may try, cannot succeed in enquiry. Therefore this fourfold *sâdhanâ* is the *sine qua non* for enquiry.

38. To begin with, a knowledge of the distinctive characteristics of these *sâdhanâs* is necessary. As already pointed out, these distinctive characteristics are categorized as cause, nature, effect, limit and fruit. These are now described.

39-44. Discernment (*viveka*) can arise only in a purified mind. Its "nature" is the conviction, gained by the help of sacred teachings, that only *Brahman* is real and all else false. Always to remember this truth is its "effect". Its end (*avadhi*) is real to be settled unwaveringly in the truth that only *Brahman* is and all else is unreal. Desirelessness (*vairâgya*) is the result of the outlook that the world is essentially false. Its "nature" is to renounce the world and have no desire for anything in it. Its "effect" is to turn away in disgust from all enjoyments as from vomit. It ends *(avadhi)* in the treatment of all pleasures, earthly or heavenly, with contempt, as if they were vomit or burning fire or hell.

Cessation of activities *(uparati)* is the outcome of the eight-fold *yoga (astânga yoga)*, namely: *yama, niyama, âsana, prânâyâma, pratyâhâra, dhâranâ, dhyâna* and *samâdhi*, i.e., self-restraint, disci-pline, steady posture, control of breath, control of senses, mind collected to truth, meditation and peace. Its "nature" consists in restraining the mind. Its "effect" is to cease from worldly activi-ties. It ends *(avadhi)* in forgetfulness of the world as if in sleep, owing to the ending of activities. Desire to be liberated *(mumuk-shutva)* begins with association with realized sages. Its "nature" is the yearning for liberation. Its "effect" is to stay with one's Master. It ends *(avadhi)* in giving up all study of *shâstras* and per-formance of religious rites.

When these have reached their limits as mentioned above, the *sâdhanas* are said to be perfect.

45-47. Should only one or more of these *sâdhanas* be perfect but not all of them, the person will after death gain celestial regions. If all of them are perfect, they together quickly make the person thoroughly capable of enquiry into the Self. Only when all the *sâdhanas* are perfect is enquiry possible, otherwise, not. Even if one of them remains undeveloped, it obstructs enquiry. With this we shall deal presently.

48-49. Dispassion, etc., remaining undeveloped, discern-ment, though perfect, cannot by itself remove the obstacles to enquiry into the Self. You see how many are well-read in *Vedânta shâstra*. They must all possess this virtue, but they have not cul-tivated the others, dispassion, etc. Therefore, they cannot undertake the enquiry into the Self. This fact makes it plain that discernment unattended by dispassion, etc., cannot avail one.

50-51. *D.:* How is it that even scholars in *Vedânta* have not suc-ceeded in the pursuit of enquiry?

M.: Though they always study *Vedânta* and give lessons to others, yet in the absence of desirelessness, they do not practice what they have learnt.

D.: And what do they do otherwise?

M.: Like a parrot they reproduce the *Vedântic* jargon but do not put the teachings into practice.

D.: What does *Vedânta* teach?

M.: The *Vedânta* teaches a man to know that all but the non-dual *Brahman* is laden with misery; therefore to leave off all desires for enjoyment; to be free from love or hate, thoroughly to cut the knot of the ego appearing as "I"; to turn away from all the illusory phenomena such as I, you, he, this, that, mine and yours; to rid oneself of the conceit of "I" and "mine"; to live unconcerned with the pairs of opposites such as heat and cold, pain and pleasure, etc.; to remain fixed in the perfect knowledge of the equality of all, making no distinction of any kind; never to be aware of anything but *Brahman,* and always to be experiencing the bliss of the non-dual Self.

Though *Vedânta* is read and well understood, if dispassion is not practiced, the desire for pleasures will not fade away. If there is no dislike for pleasing things, the desire for them cannot leave the person. Because desire is not checked, love, anger, etc., the ego or the I-conceit in the obnoxious body; the sense of possession represented by "I" or "mine", of things agreeable to the body; the pairs of opposites like pleasure and pain, and false values, will not disappear. However well read one may be, unless the teachings are put into practice, one is not really learned. Like a parrot, the man will be repeating that *Brahman* alone is real and all else is false.

D.: Why should he be so?

M.: The knowers say that like a dog delighting in offal, this man also delights in external pleasures. Though always busy with *Vedânta,* reading and teaching it, he is no better than a mean dog.

52. Having read all the *shâstras* and being well-grounded in them, they grow conceited that they are all-knowing, accomplished and worthy of respect; filled with love and hate they presume themselves respectable; they are only pack-asses esteemed for carrying loads over long distances in difficult and tortuous roads. They need not be considered as regards non-dual Truth. In the same strain Vasishtha has spoken much more to Râma.

53. *D.:* Have there been those who being well read in the *shâstras* have not practiced their teachings?

M.: Oh, many. We have also read of them in the *purânas*. Once there was a *brahmin*, Brahma Sarma by name. He was well versed in the *Vedas* and the *Vedânta* and otherwise an accomplished man too. He would not practice what he had learnt but would give lessons in it to others. Filled with love and hate, transgressing the code of conduct by acting according to greed, and otherwise enjoying himself according to his own sweet will, after death he passed to hell. For the same reason, so many more also went the same way.

In the world we see so many learned *pandits* consumed by pride and malice. No doubt a study of *Vedânta* makes one discerning. But if this is not accompanied by dispassion, etc., it is useless and does not lead to enquiry.

54-56. *D.:* Will discernment together with dispassion meet the end?

M.: No. In the absence of cessation of activities, these two are not enough for a successful pursuit of enquiry. In its absence, there will be no desire to enquire into the Self. How can we speak of success in it?

D.: What will a man with dispassion do if he does not take to enquiry into the Self?

M.: Activities not ceasing, there is no tranquility ; being desireless he dislikes all enjoyments and cannot find pleasure in home, wealth, arts, etc. ; so he renounces them, retires into solitary forests and engages in severe but fruitless austerities. The case of King Shikhidhvaja is an example of this.

57-59. *D.:* Then will discernment together with desirelessness and cessation of activities achieve the end?

M.: Not without the desire to be liberated. If this desire is wanting, there will be no incentive to enquire into the Self.

D.: What will the man be doing then?

M.: Being desireless and peaceful, he will not make any effort but remain indifferent.

D.: Have there been men with these three qualities who did not take to enquiry into the Self?

M.: Yes. Dispassion is implied in all austerities; the mind too remains one-pointed for *tapasyâ;* yet they cannot enquire into the Self.

D.: What do they do then?

M.: Averse to external pursuits, with their minds concentrated, they always remain austere in animated suspense, like that of deep sleep, but will not enquire into the Self. As an instance in point, the *Râmâyana* says of Sharabhanga *rishi* that after all his *tapasyâ* he went to heaven.

D.: Does not heaven form part of the fruits of enquiry?

M.: No. Enquiry must end in liberation, and this is freedom from repeated births and deaths which does not admit of transit from one region to another. Sharabhanga's case indicates that he could not and did not enquire into the Self. Therefore all the four qualifications are essential for enquiry.

60-61. A simple desire to be liberated unaccompanied by the other three qualities will not be enough. By an intense desire for liberation a man may take to enquiry but if otherwise unqualified, he must fail in his attempt. His case will be like that of a lame man wistfully yearning for honey in a honeycomb high up on a tree ; he cannot reach it and must remain unhappy. Or the seeker may approach a Master, surrender to him and profit by his guidance.

D.: What authority is there for saying that a man not otherwise qualified but intensely desirous of liberation remains ever unhappy?

62. *M.:* In the *Sûtra Samhitâ* it is said that those desirous of enjoyments and yet yearning for liberation, are surely bitten by the deadly serpent of *samsâra* and therefore dazed by its poison. This is the authority.

Of the view that all the four qualities must be together and in full, there is complete agreement between the *shrutis,* reason and experience. Otherwise, even if one of them is wanting, enquiry cannot be pursued to success, but after death regions of merit will be gained. When all the four qualities are perfect and together present, enquiry is fruitful.

63-69. *D.:* In conclusion, who are fit for enquiry into the Self?

M.: Only those who have all the four requisite qualities in full, are fit, and not others, whether versed in *Vedas* and *shâstras* or otherwise highly accomplished; not practitioners of severe austerities; not those strictly observing the religious rites or vows or reciting *mantras*; not worshippers of any kind; not those giving away large gifts; not wandering pilgrims, etc. Just as the *Vedic* rites are not for the unregenerate, so also enquiry is not for the unqualified.

D.: Can want of requisite qualities disqualify even a very learned scholar?

M.: Be he learned in all the sacred lore or ignorant of all of it, only the fourfold requisites can qualify a man for enquiry. The *shruti* says: "The one whose mind is in equipoise, senses controlled, whose activities have ceased and who possesses fortitude" is fit for this. From this it follows that others are not competent but only those possessing the fourfold virtues.

70. *D.:* Is any distinction made amongst seekers who are competent?

M.: For enquiry into the Self there is absolutely no distinction bearing on caste, stage of life or other similar matters. Be the seeker the foremost scholar, *pandit,* illiterate man, child, youth, old man, bachelor, householder, *tapasvi, sannyâsi, brahmin, kshatriya, vaishya, shûdra, chandâla* or woman, only these four qualifications make up the seeker. This is the undisputed view of the *Vedas* and *shâstras.*

71. *D.:* This cannot be. How can illiterate men, women and *chandâlas* be qualified to the exclusion of a *pandit* learned in the *shâstras?* He must certainly be more qualified than others. You say that a knowledge of the *shâstras* is no qualification but practice of their teachings is. No one can practice what he has not known. How can an illiterate person qualify himself in the requisite manner?

M.: In reply I ask you, and you tell me, how does the learned man qualify himself?

D.: Because he has known the teachings of the *shâstras* that he should not do *karma* for selfish ends but dedicate it to God, he will do so; his mind will be purified; gradually he will acquire the dispassion, etc., needed for enquiry. Now tell me how an illiterate man can qualify himself.

M.: He also can. Though not learned now, he might have

learnt the teachings in preceding births and done actions dedicated to God; his mind being already pure enough, he can now readily acquire the qualities needed for enquiry into the Self.

72. *D.:* In the illiterate man, should the *sâdhanâs* acquired in preceding births, and later lying as latencies, now manifest themselves, why should not his learning acquired in those births similarly manifest itself now?

M.: Some of his past *karma* may obstruct only the learning from remanifesting itself.

D.: If the learning is obstructed, how is not the *sâdhanâ* also obstructed from manifestation?

M.: Though the learning is obstructed, the fruits of his valuable labor cannot be lost ; he cannot lose his competence for enquiry.

73. *D.:* What would happen if his fourfold *sâdhanâs* were obstructed as well as his learning?

M.: The result would be that for want of the requisite qualities, neither the scholar nor the other would be fit for enquiry. Both would be equal.

74-76. *D.:* No, this cannot be. Though not already qualified, the scholar, having known the teachings, can put them into practice and gradually qualify himself, whereas the other, with all his studies, had not already succeeded in his preceding births. What hope can there be now that he has forgotten what he had learnt and his *sâdhanâs* are obstructed? Obviously he cannot be successful in enquiry.

M.: Not so. Though illiterate, a man anxious for liberation will approach a Master, learn from him the essence of the scriptures, earnestly practice the teachings and succeed in the end. Just as a worldly man ignorant of scriptures yet desirous of heaven, seeks guidance from a Master and by observance, worship and discipline, gains his end, so also by a Master's teachings even an illiterate man can certainly benefit as much as the scholar with his knowledge.

77-78. *D.:* Religious rites bear fruits only according to the earnestness of the man. Only if the seeker of Truth is earnest can a Master's guidance act in the same manner. Otherwise how can it be?

M.: Just as earnestness is the essential factor for reaping fruits from *karma,* so it is with the practice of *sâdhanâs* by the learned scholar or the Master's disciple. *Karma* or *sâdhanâ* cannot succeed if interest is wanting in them. A scholar or an illiterate man reaps the fruits of *karma* according to the interest he takes in its performance. One who is not earnest need not be considered in any matter concerning the *Vedas* or a Master.

79. A scholar or an illiterate man, if he has not already qualified himself as aforesaid, but is now desirous of liberation, should in right earnest practice the *sâdhanâs* so that he may qualify himself now at least. He will later be fit for enquiry. So no distinction can be made between a scholar and an illiterate man.

80. *D.:* If so, regarding fitness for enquiry into the Self, how does a scholar differ from an illiterate man?

M.: The difference lies only in the learning and not in the practice of *sâdhanâ* or enquiry.

81-82. *D.:* No, this cannot be. Though learning does not make any difference in *sâdhanâ,* it must certainly weigh in favor of the scholar in the pursuit of enquiry.

M.: Not so. *Shâstra* is not the means for enquiry. The means consist of desirelessness, etc. Only these can qualify a man for enquiry, and a learning of the *shâstras* does not make any difference. Therefore a scholar has no advantage over an illiterate man in the field of enquiry.

83-85. *D.:* Granted that dispassion, etc., form the means for success in enquiry. Even with the necessary *sâdhanâs,* the enquiry into the Self must be pursued only in the light of the *shâstras.* Therefore the study of the *shâstras* should be indispensable for the successful pursuit of enquiry.

M.: Nonsense! No *shâstra* is required to know the Self. Does any one look into the *shâstras* for the Self? Surely not.

D.: Only if the Self is already known, will *shâstra* not be required for enquiry into the Self. But the seeker, being deluded, has not known his true nature. How can an illiterate man realize the Self without studying the *shâstras* which deal with the nature of the Self? He cannot. Therefore the *shâstras* must be learnt as a preliminary to realization.

M.: In this case the knowledge of the Self gotten from the *shâstras* will be like that of heaven mentioned in the *Vedas,* i.e., indirect and not directly experienced. This knowledge corresponds to hearsay and cannot be direct perception. Just as knowledge of the form of Vishnu always remains indirect because there is no direct perception of the four-armed being; or again, knowledge of heaven always remains indirect in this world, so also the knowledge of the Self contained in the *shâstras* can only be indirect. This leaves the man where he was, just as ignorant as before. Only the knowledge of direct experience can be true and useful; the Self is to be realized and not to be talked about.

86-88. *D.:* Has any one said so before?

M.: Shri Vidyâranyaswâmi has said in *Dhyâna Deepika:*

The knowledge of the figure of Vishnu gained from *shâstras,* that He has four arms, is holding a disc, a conch, etc., is only indirect and cannot be direct. The description is intended to serve as a mental picture for worship and no one can see it face to face. Similarly, to know from the *shâstras* that the Self is Being-Knowledge-Bliss amounts to indirect knowledge and cannot be the same as experience. For the Self is the inmost being of the individual or the consciousness witnessing the five sheaths. It is *Brahman.* This not being realized, a superficial knowledge is all that is gained by reading the *shâstras.* It is only indirect knowledge.

D.: Vishnu or heaven, being different from the Self, can only be objective whereas the Self is subjective and its knowledge, however gained, must be only direct and cannot be indirect.

M. : Although spontaneously and directly the *Vedânta* teaches the supreme Truth, "That thou art," meaning that the inmost being of the individual is *Brahman,* yet enquiry is the only sure means of Self-realization. *Shâstric* knowledge is not enough, for it can only be indirect. Only the experience resulting from the enquiry of the Self can be direct knowledge.

89-90. Vasishtha has said the same. *Shâstra, guru* and *upadêsha* are all traditional and do not straightaway make the seeker directly realize the Self. The purity of the seeker's mind is the sole means for realization and not *shâstra* or the *guru.* The self can be realized by one's own acute discernment and no other means. All *shâstras* agree on this point.

91. From this it is clear that except by enquiry the Self can never be realized, not even by learning *Vedânta.*

92. *D.:* The Self must be realized only by a critical study of the *shâstras.* Otherwise what can be the enquiry into the Self but a critical and analytical study of the *shâstras?*

93. *M.:* In the body, senses, etc., the concept "I" persists. With one-pointed and inturned mind, to look out for this "I", or the Self, which is the inmost Being within the five sheaths, is the enquiry into the Self. To seek elsewhere outside the body by an oral recitation of *Vedânta shâstra,* or a critical study of its words, cannot be called enquiry into the Self, which can only be a thorough investigation into the true nature of the Self by a keen mind.

94-96. *D.:* Can the Self not be known by reading and understanding the *shâstras?*

M.: No. For the Self is Being-Knowledge-Bliss, different from the gross, subtle and causal bodies, witnessing the three states of waking, dream and deep sleep. Constantly exercising the vocal organs in reading the *shastras* or critically examining the scriptures and making out their meaning with a thorough knowledge of grammar, logic and diction, cannot reveal the Self which is within.

D.: How can it be realized?

M.: To examine with the mind the nature of the five sheaths; by experience to determine them; then to discard each of them step by step, "this is not the Self—this is not the Self"; and by mind grown subtle to look for the Self and realize It as the witnessing Consciousness lying beyond the five sheaths, forms the whole process. The Self cannot be seen without. It is overspread by, and lies hidden in, the five sheaths. In order to find It, the intellect must be made to turn inwards and search within, not look for It in the *shâstras.* Will any man in his senses search in a forest for a thing lost in his home? The search must be in the place where the thing lies hidden. In the same way, the Self covered over by the five sheaths must be looked for within them and not among the *shâstras.* The *shâstras* are not the place for It.

97. *D.:* True, the Self cannot be found in the *shâstras.* But

from them a scholar can learn the nature of the five sheaths, intellectually examine, experience and discard them, so as to find and realize the Self. How can the other man, ignorant of the nature of the Self or of the five sheaths, pursue the enquiry?

M.: Just as the scholar learns from books, so the other learns from the Master. Later, enquiry remains the same for both.

98-99. *D.:* Does it follow that a Master is necessary for an illiterate man and not for a scholar?

M.: Scholar or illiterate, no one can succeed without a Master. From the beginning of time, unable to realize the Self without a Master, even the seekers learned in all the *shâstras* always sought a Master to enlighten them. Nârada went to Sanatkumara; Indra to Brahmâ; Shuka to King Janaka. Unless the Master is gracious to him, no man can ever be liberated.

100-101. *D.:* Has any illiterate person been liberated by *guru*'s grace only?

M.: Yes. Yâjñavalkya helped his wife Maitreyî to be liberated. Many other women ignorant of the *shâstras*, e.g., Lîla and Chudâla were also liberated while alive. Therefore even those ignorant of the *shâstras* are qualified for enquiry into the Self.

102-108. It must now be obvious that the makeup of the best qualified seeker consists in dispassion, resulting from discernment of the real from the unreal, so that he discards all enjoyments here and hereafter as if they were poison, or vomit or blazing fire; retires from all activities to remain quiet like a man in deep sleep; but finding himself unable to remain so owing to unbearable pains, physical and mental, as if the hair of his head had caught fire and was burning, he cannot feel happy nor bear the agony even a minute longer and burns in anguish feeling, "When shall I be free? How and by what means can I be liberated ?"

For the best seeker all the qualifications must be in full, up to the abovementioned category "limit" *(avadhi)*. For the next in scale, the good seeker, the qualifications are developed only to the "effort" stage; for the middling, only to the "nature" stage; and for the lowest, only to their "cause" stage. These stages determine the success of the seeker's efforts.

109. Immediate success attends the efforts of the best quali-

fied; some time elapses before the next in grade succeeds; a longer time is required for the middling; and only a prolonged and steady practice can enable the low-grade seeker to succeed.

110-112. Their perplexity of mind does not allow the last two grades of seekers to take to enquiry. Their minds are more readily composed by *yoga,* which is more suited to them than enquiry. The first two grades of seekers readily profit by enquiry which is more suited to them than *yoga.*

113-114. In *Dhyâna Deepika,* Shri Vidyâranyaswâmi has said: The path of enquiry cannot lead seekers to success whose minds are confused. To bring down the conceit of their minds, *yoga* is necessary. The minds of those who are fully qualified are not confused but remain one-pointed; only the veiling power of ignorance still hides the Self from them; they await only awakening. Enquiry is the process of awakening; therefore it best suits them.

115-118. *Yoga* can be successful only after a long, steady, earnest, diligent and cautious practice, without needless strain.

D.: Why should one be so heedful about it?

M.: When the attempt is made to fix the mind in the Self, it gets restive and drags the man through the senses to the objects. However resolute and learned the man may be, his mind remains wayward, strong, mulish, and hard to restrain. Wanton by nature, it cannot remain steady for a moment; it must run here, there and everywhere; now it dwells in the nether regions and in a trice it flies up in the sky; it moves in all the directions of the compass; and it is capricious like a monkey. It is hard to fix. To do so, one must be heedful.

119-121. In the (*Bhagavad*) *Gîtâ,* Arjuna asked Shri Bhagavân: "O Krishna! Is not the mind always capricious, disturbing to the man and too strong to be checked? It is easier to hold the air in the fist than to control the mind."

In the *Yoga* Vasishtha, Shri Râma asked Vasishtha: "O Master! Is it not impossible to control the mind? One may sooner drink up the oceans, or lift up Mt. Meru or swallow flaming fire than control the mind." From the words of Râma and Arjuna, and our own experience, there can be no doubt that it is exceedingly difficult to control the mind, however able and heroic one may be.

122-124. *D.:* Control of mind being so difficult, how can *yoga* be practiced at all?

M.: By dint of practice and dispassion, the mind can be brought under control. The same has been said by Shri Bhagavân to Arjuna and by Vasishtha to Shri Râma. Shri Krishna said: "O son of Kunti! There is no doubt that the mind is wayward and difficult to control. Nevertheless by dint of practice and dispassion it can be controlled." Vasishtha said: "O Râma, though the mind is hard to control, yet it must be subdued by dispassion and effort, even at the cost of wringing your hands, clenching your teeth and holding down the senses and limbs; it must be accomplished by willpower."

Therefore, intense effort is necessary for the purpose.

125-127. The honeybee of the mind, ever living in the lotus of the heart, turns away from the sweet honey of unequalled bliss of the heart-lotus, and desirous of honey bitter with misery, collected outside as sound, touch, form, taste and smell, always flies out through the senses. Though by dispassion the senses are forcibly closed and the mind shut in, yet remaining within, it will be thinking of the present, or recollecting the past or building castles in the air.

D.: How can its subtle activities also be checked and the mind completely subdued?

M: Checking its external activities and confining it within, this bee of the mind must be made to be drunk with the honey of the heart-lotus, i.e., the bliss of the Self.

128. *D.:* Please explain this *yoga*.

M : With an intense desire for liberation; reaching a *guru*; hearing from him the non-dual *Brahman* shining forth as Being-Knowledge-Bliss of the Self; understanding It, though indirectly, yet as clearly as one understands Vishnu, etc.; turning the mind one-pointedly to this *Brahman*, without taking to enquiry by reflection (*manana*); always meditating on the non-dual Self of Being-Knowledge-Bliss, attributeless and un-differentiated, is called *yoga*. By its practice the mind becomes tranquil and can gradually go to *samâdhi*. In *samâdhi* it will experience the supreme Bliss.

129-130. *D.:* Has any other said so before?

49

M.: Yes. Shri Bhagavân has said: The *yogi* who, controlling the mind, always turns it upon the Self, becomes perfectly calm and ultimately gains Me, i.e., the bliss of liberation. The mind of the *yogi* who always practices *yoga,* will be steady like a flame protected from the breeze, and, without movement, will pass into *samâdhi.*

131-133. Similarly, by enquiry, the mind readily gains peace and *samâdhi.* .

D.: What is this enquiry?

M.: After hearing from the *guru* about the nature of the Self, which in the *shâstras* is spoken of as *Brahman* or Being-Knowledge-Bliss, to gain a clear indirect knowledge; then according to *upadesha* and by intelligent reasoning to enquire and find out the Self which is pure Knowledge, and the non-self which is objective and insentient like the ego; to discern and sift them; then directly to experience them as different from each other; later on, by meditation, to extinguish all that is objective, and to absorb into the Self the residual mind left over as non-dual, ends in the direct experience of supreme Bliss. Here it has been described in brief, but the *shâstras* deal with it elaborately.

134. This chapter on *sâdhanâ* has dealt with these two means, enquiry and *yoga,* for making the mind still. According to his merits an intelligent seeker should practice either of them.

135. This chapter is meant for the earnest student in order that he may study carefully and analyze his qualifications to ascertain what he already has and what more is wanted. After properly equipping himself he can find out which of these two methods suits him and then practice it till success.

Chapter IV

Shravana

Hearing

1. In the foregoing chapter we have seen that *yoga* is suited to the lower grade of seekers and enquiry to the higher. In this chapter we shall consider the path of enquiry which effortlessly leads to knowledge of *Brahman*.

2-4. *D.:* What is this path of enquiry?

M.: From the *shâstras* it is well-known to Consist of *shravana, manana, nididhyâsana* and *samâdhi*, i.e., hearing the Truth, reflection, meditation and blissful Peace. The *Vedas* themselves declare it to be so. "My dear, the Self must be heard from the Master, reflected and meditated upon." In another place it is said that in blissful Peace the Self must be realized. The idea has been repeated by Lord Shri Shankarâchârya in his *Vâkyavritti*, namely that until the meaning of the sacred text "I am Brahman" is realized in all its true significance, one must be practicing *shravana*, etc.

5-7. In *Chitra Deepika*, Shri Vidyâranyaswâmi has said that enquiry is the means to knowledge and it consists in hearing the Truth, reflection and meditation; only the state of blissful Peace of awareness, in which *Brahman* alone exists and nothing else, is the true "nature" of knowledge; the non-revival of the knot of the ego parading as "I", which has been lost once for all, is its "effect"; always to remain fixed as "I am the Supreme Self" just as strongly, unequivocally and unerringly as the heretofore ignorant identification "I am the body" is its "end"; liberation is its "fruit". From this it follows that only hearing, etc., is the enquiry into the Self.

8-10. To hear the supreme Truth, reflect and meditate on it, and to remain in *samâdhi* form together the enquiry into the

51

Self. They have for their "'cause'" *(hetu)* the aforesaid four *sâd-hanâs*, namely, discernment, desirelessness, tranquillity and desire to be liberated. Which of these is essential for which part of enquiry will be mentioned in its appropriate place. Here we shall deal with *shravana*.

M.: *Shravana* consists in ascertaining, by means of the six proofs considered together, that the *Vedas* aim at the non-dual *Brahman* only.

11-12. To analyze *shravana* under the five categories:

Intense desire to be liberated gives rise to it; always to be hearing of the non-dual *Brahman* is its "nature"; the complete removal of that aspect of the veiling power of ignorance which says, "It (*Brahman*) does not exist" is its "effect"; non-recurrence of this veiling power is its "limit"; a firm indirect knowledge is its "fruit."

13. *D.:* How can the desire to be liberated be said to be its "cause"?

M.: In the *shruti* it is said, "In the state of dissolution before creation there was only the non-dual Reality." This Reality is the same as the Self. Only he who is eager to be liberated will seek the knowledge of the Self and take to hearing it. No other is interested in It. Therefore eagerness to be liberated is the essential requisite for this part of enquiry, namely *shravana*.

14. *D.:* Just now you said that always to be hearing of the non-dual Self is the "nature" of *shravana*. Who is this non-dual Self?

M.: He is famous in the *shrutis* as the Consciousness beyond the gross, subtle and causal bodies, apart from the five sheaths, and the witness of the waking, dream and sleep states.

15-17. *D.:* What can be beyond the gross, subtle and causal bodies?

M.: Of these the gross body is composed of skin, blood, muscles, fat, bones, nerve-stuff and lymph ; it is secreting and excreting; it is born and dies; like a wall it is insentient; like a pot it is an object of the senses.

The subtle body is the internal organ *(antahkarana)* well known as the mind, which functions as the I-mode and "this"-mode; together with the five vital airs, the five senses and the five organs and limbs, it transmigrates to other bodies or worlds;

always remaining within a gross body it experiences pleasures and pains.

The beginningless, neither real nor unreal, and indescribable ignorance manifests these subtle and gross bodies and is therefore said to be the causal body.

18. These three bodies are contrary to the nature of the Self.
D.: How?

M.: The gross body is insentient; the subtle is pain-ridden; the causal is unreal. These are the opposites of the Being-Knowledge-Bliss nature of the Self. Therefore the Self must be different from these.

19-25. *D.:* How is it different from the five sheaths also?

M.: The five sheaths are the material, the vital, the mental, the intellectual and the blissful. Of these the material sheath is born of food and grows with food; it is thus food-modified. Therefore it is material. Like a sheath to a sword, the body covers the Self and obstructs its knowledge. Therefore it is the material sheath. Moreover it has a beginning and an end. Therefore it is not the Self, who is eternal. The vital, the mental and the intellectual sheaths together form the subtle body. Through the five passages in the body, functioning in five different ways according to its modes, the vital airs together with the five organs and limbs obstruct the Self from being known. therefore, this is the vital sheath. Being insentient, it cannot be the Self.

Joined with desire, anger, etc., thinking this and that, the "this"-mode of mind manifests the latencies. Together with the five senses the "this"-mode forms the mental sheath. Being insentient, it cannot be the Self.

Definitely to make out the "this" and "that" ideas of the mind to be a pot, a cloth, etc., to have the conceit of "I" in the body, etc., and that of "mind", in home, wealth, lands etc., is the nature of the I-mode. United with the five senses, this I-mode forms the intellectual sheath. Arising in the waking and dream states, joined with the body, permeating it from head to foot, it is resolved in swoons or in the deep sleep state. Therefore, it cannot be the eternal Self.

After waking from deep sleep, every one feels, "I did not

know anything; I slept happily." Here ignorance and bliss are the experiences. This blissful ignorance is the blissful sheath. Being ignorant, it must be insentient and non-self.

So far all the five sheaths have been shown to be non-self. The experiencer of them must be different from them like the seer of a pot remaining different from it. There can be no doubt on this point.

26. *D.:* How is the Self said to be witnessing the three states?

M.: The three states are the waking, dream and deep sleep, through which the *jîva* or the I-conceit, or the ego passes, identifying itself with the gross, subtle and causal bodies respectively. The Self must therefore be the Consciousness witnessing these three states; it is not identical with any, or all, of them.

27. *D.:* If these three states are not of the Self, of whom else can they be?

M.: They can be only of the ego which assumes them, whereas the Self is unconcerned. Affecting the waking state, the ego in the guise of *vishva,* enjoys the gross sense-experiences; similarly in dream as *taijasa* he enjoys the subtle experiences; and in deep sleep as *prâjña* he experiences ignorance. Therefore, the ego must be the experiencer in these states, and not the witnessing Self.

28-29. *D.:* What makes you say that the ego and not the Self is the experiencer of the three states?

M.: In deep sleep, the ego becoming dormant, no experience or experiencer is seen; only on the rise of the ego are they found. He must therefore be the experiencer. His are the two states of waking and dream; they cannot be those of the Self.

D.: Whose is deep sleep then?

M.: It is also of the ego, because just as it arrogates to itself the waking and dream states saying "I woke up; I dreamt", so it does the deep sleep state also, saying "I slept". It cannot be of the Self since It remains unconcerned as the witness of the three states and of their experiencer, who remains conceited with the ideas "I woke up; I dreamt; I slept." Therefore, none of the three states is of the Self.

30-31. *D.:* The ego cannot be the experiencer in deep sleep also. It is not there so how can it be said to be the experiencer?

In the waking and dream states, the ego is rightly said to be the experiencer; in deep sleep the Self must be the experiencer.

M.: You are not right. The *jîva*, i.e., the ego, who in the waking and dream states appears as the intellectual sheath to enjoy gross and subtle things, sinks in deep sleep to remain dormant as the blissful sheath, experiencing ignorance and bliss as "I did not know anything; I slept happily." Had the ego not been present in deep sleep, on waking there could not be the recollection: "I did not know anything; I slept happily". Only the experiencer can recollect his experiences, and not another. Even the recollection can only be of what was actually experienced and not of what was not. On waking it is the ego which says, "I did not know anything; I slept happily." From this it is clear that the experiencer in the deep sleep was the ego and not the Self.

32-33. *D.:* But for the blissful sheath of deep sleep what can the witnessing Consciousness be?

M.: As the blissful sheath, it is ignorant; this ignorance is recognized later. The recognizer must be different from recognition and he must be the experiencer of the blissful sheath.

Now that he has fancied himself as the blissful sheath, which is no other than ignorance, he remains ignorant himself because ignorance cannot know itself. Therefore, it follows there must be the witness of this ignorance who simply illuminates the blissful sheath which appears as the idea, "I do not know anything", and remains apart from it. This witness is the Self.

D.: What evidence is there to prove that in deep sleep all is reduced to dormancy leaving the witness unaffected?

M.: The *shruti* says: "The vision of the Witness can never be lost," meaning that when all else remains dormant and unknown, the Seer remains aware as ever.

34-35. *D.:* Well, in deep sleep which is itself ignorance, a cognizer is rightly inferred; but in the waking and dream states the intellectual sheath can be the cognizer and there is no place for a witness apart.

M.: You cannot think so. Just as in deep sleep the Self is the cognizer of the ignorance, so also in the other states it is the witness of the intellect, knowing all waking and dream notions such as, "I dreamt; I woke up; I went; I came; I saw; I heard; I know," which clearly indicate a knower. Just as the witness is admitted to be aware of ignorance, so also it must be of knowledge as well. Moreover, being a knower at one time, and not a knower at another time, the intellectual sheath cannot be the witness.

D.: If so, let the Self, the witness of the intellect, be also the experiencer.

M.: No, no! The witness of deep sleep and of its experiencer, cannot be the experiencer of the waking and dream states.

D.: If the Self be the witness of deep sleep and of its experiencer, can It not be the experiencer of the waking and dream states?

M.: No, he who sleeps must wake up or dream dreams. Never sleeping, ever aware as the Witness of the three states, and of their experiencer who thinks "I slept; I dreamt; I woke up," the Self cannot have the three states nor be their experiencer. This cannot admit of any doubts.

36. *D.:* Why should not the Self be both witness and experiencer of the three states?

M.: Just as the witness watching two men fighting with each others does not fight himself, so also the witness cannot be the experiencer. Again, as the fighter does not simply watch the fight but himself fights, so also the experiencer cannot be the witness. Therefore, the same Self cannot be both the experiencer and the witness.

D.: Now what is the conclusion?

M.: The I-conceit is the experiencer and the other one who is unconcernedly watching the states and their experiencer is the witness.

37. *D.:* In that case, for the three states are there three different witnesses or is there only one?

M.: The witness is only one whereas the states alternate one with another ; the Witness does not change. The same continuous awareness runs through the appearance, subsistence and disappearance of the three states. Thus the witness of the three states is the Self. The witnesshood of the Self has thus been described.

38. In this manner the *tatastha lakshana* of the Self has been described. Now we shall consider its *svarûpa lakshana*. It is Being-Knowledge-Bliss, single, all-permeating, untainted, perfect, unchanged and non-dual.

39-41. *D.:* What is meant by Its "Being"?

M.: It always remains witnessing the appearance and disappearance of all the states superimposed on It. Nay more: It was the Witness not only of the waking, dream and deep sleep states but also of the births, growths (childhood, youth, old age) and deaths of previous bodies (just as it is of this body and will be of future bodies). It is thus the one, continuous, ever-existent witness of all of these. Its "Being" is thus obvious.

42. *D.:* What is meant by Its being "Knowledge"?

M.: Inasmuch as It always remains illumining and manifesting the three states and their relative I-conceits, Knowledge is self-evident.

43-46. *D.:* What is meant by Its being "Bliss"?

M.: Always being the one object of Supreme joy, rather supreme joy itself, the Self is Bliss.

D.: Is not the non-self also pleasing?

M.: No.

D.: Why not?

M.: Not by itself, but only as an object of enjoyment for the individual self, the non-self is dear as husband, wife, child, wealth, home, pleasing unguents, sweet scents etc.

D.: Why are they said to be not pleasing by themselves?

M.: Should they be so, they must always remain so. At one time, one thing is pleasing and at other times, the same thing is nauseating.

D.: How?

M.: Take a woman, for instance. When the man is lustful, she is fancied to be pleasing; when he suffers from fever, she is not wanted; for a man grown desireless, she is of no interest at all. According to circumstances the same woman can be pleasing, unwanted, or of no interest. The same applies to all other objects of enjoyment. Thus the non-self cannot be pleasing.

47. *D.:* Is the Self always pleasing?

M.: Certainly. Never do you know it to be otherwise.

48-49. *D.:* In case of unbearable pain, the Self is given up in disgust. How can it be said to be always pleasing?

M.: The Self can never be given up because he, who in disgust, relinquishes the sufferings that are alien to him, does not give up himself.

D.: It is the Self that is given up by himself.

M.: In that case, if the Self is given up, there must be another who gives it up. On the other hand he being the one who gives up, gives up the painful body which is different from himself, and not himself. Furthermore the very fact of occasional disgust with the body etc., proves that the non-self is painful and the Self joyful.

D.: How does it prove this?

M.: Should the Self be painful, pain could never be disliked. Because one's true nature is joy, one dislikes pain in the shape of body, etc. Not being natural, but only adventitious, ailments are not liked. Had they been natural, they could not be disliked. Just as the dislike of illness, etc., shows that they are not natural but only adventitious, so also the dislikes of the body, etc., shows that these are similarly not natural and that joy is one's true and eternal nature. Therefore a sudden and intense disgust with the body, etc., makes a man rid himself of them but not of the Self. This very fact teaches that the body, etc., are not the Self. It must now be obvious how the Self can never be the object of dislike to any one.

50-51. *D.:* Even if the Self cannot be detested, can it not be an object of indifference?

M.: No. Being oneself the one who is indifferent, one can be indifferent to the non-self, e.g. a pebble or a blade of grass, but not to oneself. Therefore the Self is not an object of occasional dislike like the body, women, etc., nor of indifference like a blade of grass or a pebble. Always It is Joy itself.

52-53. *D.:* If the Self is always pleasing and so are sense-objects at the time of enjoyment, let them also be regarded as pleasing.

M.: The delight in any object is not lasting but what is now delightful soon yields its place to another more so. There are degrees of pleasure and succession of the objects liked. The pleasure in objects is only wanton and not steady. This is possible only if the pleasure is born of one's own delusion and not of the intrinsic value of the object. For example, see how a dog chews a dry, marrowless bone until blood comes out of the wounds in its mouth, and fancies the taste of its own blood to be that of the marrow of the bone and will not part with it. Should it find another similar bone, it drops down the one in its mouth and takes the other. In the same way, superimposing his own joyful nature on the detestable objects of fancy the man delights in them by mistake, for joy is not their nature. Owing to the ignorance of man, the objects which are really painful by nature seem to be pleasing. This seeming pleasure does not remain steady in one object but often shifts to other objects; it is wanton, graded, and not absolute, whereas the joy of the Self is not captious. Even when the body, etc., are cast off, this joy endures in the Self forever; it is also absolute. Therefore the Self is supreme Bliss. So far the Being-Knowledge-Bliss nature of the Self has been established.

54. *D.:* Do these three—Being, Knowledge and Bliss form the qualities or the nature of the Self?

M.: These are not qualities but the very Self. Just as heat, light, and redness form the nature of fire and are not its qualities, so also Being, Knowledge and Bliss are the nature of the Self.

55. *D.:* If the Self has three forms as Being, Knowledge and Bliss, are there then three selves?

M.: No, It is only one. Just as the fire showing forth as heat, light and redness, is not three but only one, or water appearing as coldness, fluidity and taste is only one, so also the Self shining forth as Being-Knowledge-Bliss is not three but only one.

56-58. *D.:* If the Self is only one, how can it be said to be all-permeating?

M.: It is correct to say that the Self, being only one, is all-permeating. Because It is all-knowing, It—as Knowledge—can permeate all.

D.: Being the inmost Self aware of the five sheaths of the body, can It be all-knowing?

M.: Yes, It can. The whole universe made up of the five elements, their combinations and mutations, is seen by It and by no other. Being insentient, the others cannot know. Otherwise the insentient, like a pot, etc., should be knowing; but it is not so. Only It knows all of them, but they do not know It. It is the all-knower.

D.: The Self perceives only such things as are within the ken of the senses and not those beyond. Where does It perceive Mt. Meru or heaven?

M.: It knows all. In the Self which is but the ether of knowledge, all that is non-self, i.e., insentient, appears in both manners, as perceived or unperceived. Just as in the ether of knowledge and not elsewhere, the home, lands, village, town and country seem perceived by the senses, so also things beyond the senses such as Mt. Meru or heaven appear as unperceived by them.

D.: Can anything unperceived by the senses appear at all?

M.: Yes, it can. Though non-existent, like the son of a barren woman, yet in the ether of Knowledge, the home, etc., appear as objects of perception because the latencies of the mind present themselves so. In the same manner, though unreal and unperceived, Mt. Meru, etc., are fancied by the mind and appear in the ether of Knowledge.

D.: How?

M.: Before the witnessing consciousness in dreams, the mental phenomena present themselves as objects of perception such as the home, etc., and also others beyond perception like heaven, etc. In the same way they do so in the waking state too. Otherwise one cannot say, "I do not know heaven, Mt. Meru, etc." However, one says, "I do not know heaven, Mt. Meru, etc." This means that heaven, Mt. Meru, etc., appear as objects unperceived by the senses. Thus the Self which knows all the insentient non-self, like Mt. Meru, etc., is this Self only.

If not found in all (everywhere) but seen only within, as the inner Self witnessing the five sheaths, how can It know all? Certainly It cannot do so. In itself the mind fancies things far and near, perceptible and imperceptible, known and unknown. As their substratum the Self runs through and knows them all. The Self is thus all-pervading. Therefore the same Self only is in all and there can be no doubt of this.

59. *D.:* Should the Self be all-pervading, It must be associated with all and therefore tainted.

M.: No. Like the all-permeating ether, It is impartite and therefore unassociated. Not only untainted like the ether, but also surpassing it, the Self remains as the ether of Consciousness. Therefore the *shrutis* say, "This *Purusha* is certainly untainted."

60. *D.:* Being unassociated and thus untainted, beyond all, separate and indifferent, the Self must be imperfect.

M.: No. There exists nothing different nor similar to It; there are no parts in It. It remains undifferentiated externally and internally. It is Perfection. Though all-filling, yet It remains unassociated like the ether.

D.: How can It be all-permeating yet impartite?

M.: Not here nor there, but all-pervading, It is undivided in space. Not now, nor then, but ever-present, It is undivided in time. There is nothing beside the Self, It is the all-Self or the very being of everything; therefore It is undivided by anything. It remains thus undivided by any or all these three, all-filling and perfect. Thus Its Perfection is proved.

61. *D.:* Because all-pervading like the ether, the Self fills all, It must be changeful.

M.: No. Being the witness of all created elements, ether, etc., that undergo changes, such as existence, birth, growth, transformation, decay and death, the Self cannot Itself be changeful. Otherwise, like the other things, It would be changing; then It must be born, grow and die away. Thus, It would fall into the category of insentient things. If insentient, It cannot at all be aware. On the contrary, It is known always to remain as the witness of the birth, growth and decay of all the universe. It is also impartite. Therefore It must be free from changes.

62-63. *D.:* To say that the Self is free from changes implies the existence of non-self which is changing. Then the Self cannot be "non-dual" and duality must result.

M.: No. There exists nothing besides the Self. It is "non-dual". If the non-self is not different from the Self, there cannot be duality.

D.: How can the non-self be the Self and not separate from the Self?

M.: The Self is the origin of all. The effect cannot be different from its cause. We do not see them totally different from each other. Being the cause of all, the Self is identical with all. There can be nothing different from It.

64-66. D.: How can the Self be the origin of all?

M.: Being the seer of all, It is the origin of all.

D.: How can the seer be the origin?

M.: In all cases of illusion, only the seer is found to be the cause of all of them. When nacre is seen to be silver, the material cause is no other than the seer; the same is the case with all dream-visions for they have their origin in the dreamer only. Similarly with the illusion of the world of the waking state, the seer must be the cause.

D.: Should the universe be a fiction, your conclusion will follow. Is this universe only a fiction?

M.: First, there is the authority of the *shrutis* which say that in dissolution there remains only the non-dual Self; and in creation the names and forms are superimposed on It by *Mâyâ* like the name and form of a snake on a dimly visible rope.

Second, reasoning shows the illusory nature of this universe because it is seen to appear and disappear like the unreal visions in dreams.

Third, the sages have proclaimed in their realization that all this is but illusory and that only *Brahman* is real.

Therefore all this universe is really false. Now it is but right to say that being the witness, the Self is the sole cause of all this universe, which is but an illusory appearance on the Self. The illusory effect cannot be separate from the basis. Just as the foam, bubbles and waves are not different from their origin, the sea, so also the phenomena of the Universe are but the Self falsely presented. Therefore the Self is "non-dual" and there can be no duality.

67. In the presence of the Master to ever-attentively study the *Vedânta shâstra*, which treats of the non-dual Being, and retain its meaning, forms the "nature" of *shravana* or hearing. This must always be attended to.

68. *D.:* What is the "effect" of this *shravana?*

M.: It destroys that veiling part of ignorance which hitherto made one think: "Where is this non-dual Self? Nowhere". To destroy this ignorant conclusion of the non-existence of the non-dual Self is its "effect".

69-70. *D.:* How long should one continue *shravana?*

M.: Until the doubt of the non-existence of the non-dual Being does not rear its head again. The non-recurrence of the doubt is said to be the "limit" of the process of *shravana.*

D.: Can the doubt, once set at rest, recur?

M.: Yes, it can.

D.: How?

M.: In many passages in the *shrutis,* duality is dealt with, and can easily be mistaken to be proved. For instance, one studies the *shâstras* dealing with Vishnu and becomes devoted to Him; later on, finding other gods similarly dealt with, one's devotion to Vishnu is likely to suffer. In the same manner, a study of the *Advaita shâstras* removes the doubt regarding the non-dual Being, yet the *Advaita shâstras* may lead to a different conclusion and the student may lose faith in the non-duality of Being. Therefore, one must continue *shravana* until the different texts do not shake one's reasoned faith in non-dual Being.

D.: What is the "fruit" of *shravana?*

M.: When once for all the non-belief in the non-duality of Being is destroyed, no sacred text or tricky argument can make the seeker deviate from his faith. All obstructions to his faith thus removed, he remains steady in his indirect knowledge of non-dual Being. This is the "fruit" of *shravana.*

71. *D.:* What is this indirect knowledge?

M.: To know the true nature of the inmost Self, not by direct experience but by a study of the *shâstras,* is called indirect knowledge. Although one does not see Vishnu face to face yet through the evidence of the *shâstras* one believes in His existence; this forms only common *(sâmânya)* knowledge. Similarly, a common knowledge of non-duality of *Brahman* gained through the *Advaita shâstras* is indirect knowledge.

72-76. *D.:* Why should the knowledge arising from *shravana* be said to be indirect? Can it not be direct?

M.: No. So long as the inner Self cannot shine forth owing to the other veiling aspect of ignorance *(abhânâvarana)* mere knowledge of Its existence cannot be called direct.

D.: Is this confirmed by others also?

M.: Yes. Shri Vidyâranyaswâmi says in *Dhyâna Deepika:*

"Though by *shravana, Brahman* can be understood to be Being-Knowledge-Bliss, yet It cannot thus be directly experienced as the sole Being witnessing the five sheaths. Although from the *shâstras,* Vishnu is understood to be four-armed, holding a disc, a conch and a mace in His hands, and even a mental picture of Him can manifest in one-pointed meditation, yet He is not seen directly with these eyes; therefore the knowledge of Him remains only indirect." The knowledge gained from the *shâstras* is thus only indirect and not directly experienced. Similarly, the knowledge gained by *shravana* can remain only indirect and is not directly experienced.

D.: Here Vishnu is not the Self but is different. It is but right that knowledge of Him gained from the *shâstras* remains indirect. But *Brahman* is not different from the Self. To the seeker who is ignorant of this identity, the *shrutis* reveal the fact saying, "That thou art". On learning its true significance he should be said to have directly realized the Truth. This knowledge cannot remain indirect like that of heaven, etc. *Shravana* must therefore end in directly experienced knowledge.

M.: Not so. It is true that the sacred text reveals the Truth, "That thou art". Still, direct knowledge does not result merely by hearing it. In the absence of enquiry into the Self, knowledge cannot become direct. In order to have this indirect knowledge directly experienced, it is necessary to reflect on it.

77. Here ends the chapter on *shravana.* The student who reads this carefully will gain indirect knowledge. In order to experience directly, he will seek to know the nature of *manana,* or reflection.

Chapter V

Manana

Reflection

1. *D.:* Master, on hearing it from you, the nature of the Self is now clear to me, but the knowledge remains only indirect. Kindly instruct me in reflection, by practicing which, the darkness of ignorance now hiding the Self may vanish and direct experience may result.

2. *M.:* Always to direct thought, with subtle reasoning upon the non-dual Self that is now known indirectly, is called reflection.

3-4. *D.:* Please tell me its "cause," "nature," "effect," "limit," and "fruit".

M.: Discernment of the real from the unreal is its "cause"; enquiry into the Truth of the non-dual Self is its "nature"; to tear off that veiling aspect of ignorance which makes one say, "It does not shine forth," is its "effect"; the non-recrudescence of this veiling is its "limit"; and direct experience is its "fruit". So say the sages.

D.: Why is discernment said to be its "cause"?

M.: Only he who, by discernment of the real from the unreal has acquired indirect knowledge, is fit to seek by enquiry the direct knowledge of experience. No other can succeed in the search for it.

6. *D.:* Why should not the desire for liberation be the "cause" of reflection?

M.: A mere desire to be liberated cannot make a man fit for enquiry into the Self. Without *shravana* one cannot have even an indirect knowledge. How can one succeed in one's enquiry? Only after knowing the nature of the Self should one proceed to seek It. Ignorant of Its true nature, how can one investigate the Self? Simple desire to be liberated will not suffice.

7. *D.:* Should not this desire lead to enquiry? With the rise of this desire the man will begin to hear about the nature of the Self and gain indirect knowledge which must enable him to undertake the enquiry.

M.: This amounts to saying that the seeker possesses discernment. He is not only desirous of Liberation but also discerning in intellect. With *shravana* comes this faculty of intellectual discernment of the real from the unreal, or the Self from the non-self. This is called indirect knowledge. The *shâstras* say that only he who possesses indirect knowledge can discern the real or the Self from the unreal or the non-self, and is fit for enquiry into the Self. Therefore, discernment is the *sine qua non* for enquiry.

8-12. *D.:* Even if the desire for liberation be not the particular *(vishesha)* cause of reflection, could not either desirelessness or tranquility be the cause of it?

M.: All these are only general aids for reflection but not its particular causes. A desireless and tranquil man need not necessarily have the indirect knowledge of the Self and is therefore unfit for enquiry into the Self. There are men of austerities who are desireless and tranquil but not anxious for liberation. Having no desire for liberation they have not heard at all about the Self.

D.: How can they be said not to be desirous of liberation?

M.: Inasmuch as they engage in austerities without taking to *shravana,* etc., which is the only gateway to liberation, the absence of the desire for liberation is inferred.

D.: No, they too can be desirous of being liberated.

M.: If so, they must give up their austerities, always remain with a Master and engage themselves in hearing of the Self. If it be said that they have already done *shravana* also, then since they will have gained indirect knowledge, they should be engaged in reflection. Not having done *shravana,* though endowed with desirelessness and tranquility, they are incapable of discerning the real from the unreal and therefore unit for enquiry into the Self. Desirelessness, etc., can only be aids to this enquiry but not its chief causes. Discernment of the real from the unreal is the only chief cause.

13-14. *D.:* Can the Self not be realized by austerities, accompanied by desirelessness and tranquility, and without enquiry?

M.: No. By non-enquiry, the Self has been lost sight of; to regain It, enquiry is needed. In its absence, how can even crores of austerities restore the sight? Always to enquire into the Self is the only remedy for the blindness of the ignorant whose mental eye has been bedimmed by the darkness of non-enquiry spreading its veil. Except by the eye of knowledge, gained through enquiry, the Self cannot be realized.

15-16. *D.:* What is this enquiry into the Self?

M.: With one-pointed intellect to seek within the five sheaths the Self which is shining forth as "I" in the body, senses, etc., considering "Who is this Self? Where is It?" and "How is It?" is the nature of the enquiry into the Self. With subtle intellect the enquiry into the Real, namely the Self within the unreal sheaths, must always be pursued.

17. *D.:* Earlier it was said that the Self is all-permeating. How can the all-permeating Self be looked for only in the sheaths? Moreover the sheaths are said to be unreal. How can an enquiry into unreal things lead to the recognition of the Real?

18-19. *M.:* Truly the Self is all-permeating. Still Its knowledge is obscured by the covering of the five sheaths.

The Self which lies hidden in them must be looked for only there and not elsewhere. A thing is sought in the place where it was lost. Something lost at home is not looked for in a forest. In the same manner the Self hidden in the five sheaths, and remaining unrecognized by wrong identification with them, must be found only by sifting the unwanted elements, here the five sheaths.

D.: How can an investigation into unreal things lead to the recognition of the Real?

M.: The unreal coverings must be removed to disclose the Real hidden in them. They are superimposed on the real Self. They must be examined and ascertained to be unreal so that their substratum, which is the sole Real, can be known. Unless the external trappings that are superimposed are looked into, their substratum, i.e. the Real, cannot be found. Has anyone in the world been able to find the rope without looking and enquiring into the nature of the seeming snake, though this is superimposed on it and unreal? Or can there be anyone, who having enquired into the superimposed snake, did not discover its substratum to be the rope? No one. In the same manner an indirect knowledge should be gained, by *shravana*, that the five sheaths are superimposed and unreal; but by a keen intellect the seeker must probe deep into this superficial knowledge and experience the truth of it. Just as the directly experienced gross body is clearly known to be built up by food and recognized to be only the food-sheath covering the Self, so also the other four subtler sheaths remaining unknown to the common people, but taught by the scriptures and the Master, must be known by their characteristics; they must be enquired into and directly experienced. At the same time they must be recognized to be only sheaths and successively dismissed in order to seek their witness: Consciousness-Being or the subtle Self.

20. *D.:* If the Self is enquired into, after investigation and the dismissal of these sheaths, how can It be realized?

M.: This enquiry is but the reflection on the Self, i.e., *manana*; its effect is to destroy the veil of ignorance. A constant reflection on the Self lying behind the sheaths must burn away that aspect of veiling which makes one say, "It does not shine forth".

D.: How can this be?

M.: Just as an enquiry into the rope-snake that obstructs the rope from view destroys the ignorance of the rope, so also a keen quest for the Self that remains as the witness of the five sheaths, destroys the ignorance which supposes that the Self is not seen and that It does not shine forth. As clouds are scattered away when the sun shines forth in its full glory and the darkness of veiling is destroyed, even so will the witnessing Self shine forth in all Its splendor. Therefore enquiry is necessary.

21. *D.:* How long should one continue enquiry into the Self?

M.: Non-recrudescence of the darkness of ignorance is said to be the "limit" of reflection. Therefore one should continue the practice until this darkness of ignorance does not recur.

22-24. D.: Can the veiling, once removed, return again?

M.: Yes. So long as doubts arise, this ignorance must be

inferred to exist.

D.: How can there be any doubt left after the Self has been realized?

M.: On enquiring into the sheaths and dismissing them as unreal, the Self, their witnessing consciousness, is realized to be unique, finer than ether, even like a void. Now that the sheaths have been dismissed as unreal and there is nothing but the void-like subtle Self, a fear may arise that one is left as nothing or void.

D.: How can it be?

M.: Transcending all, the Self has nothing in common with worldly things or activities. It transcends the void also; hence, the experience is unique and unearthly. A fear may then arise: "Can this be the Self? It cannot be. Should this be the Self, how can I be such a void?" Even after realizing the impartite Self, there is no confidence in one's own experience; it is regarded as impossible and a great doubt arises. The sense of impossibility gives rise to doubt. But repeated reflection removes this sense of impossibility. So it is said by Vyâsa in the *Brahma Sutras*: "On account of the repeated instruction (by the scriptures), (it is) necessary repeatedly (to hear of, reflect and meditate on the Self)."

25. *D.:* What is the "fruit" of such reflection?

M.: By continued practice, the veiling is destroyed; with its destruction, the sense of impossibility of the Self shining forth all alone disappears; with its disappearance all obstacles are at an end and then direct experience results as clearly and surely as an apple in the palm of your hand. This is the "fruit".

26. *D.:* What is this direct experience?

M.: Just as one can clearly distinguish the sun from the cloud hiding it, so also when one can distinguish the Self from the ego, it is direct experience. This is the "fruit" of reflection.

27. My son, wise boy, reflection has now been taught in detail. It is for you to enquire into the five sheaths, dismiss them as unreal and, with intellect turned inwards, to find the very subtle Self, and recognize it distinctively.

28. *D.:* O Master, even on a keen enquiry I am unable to say, "These are the five sheaths; this is the inmost Self as distin-

guished from them." I cannot directly realize the Self. Why is it so?

M.: This is owing to beginningless ignorance.

D.: How did this ignorance arise?

M.: From the aforesaid veiling.

D.: How?

M.: Although by nature the Self and the ego are quite different from each other, the aforesaid veiling presents them as if they were identical.

D.: Please explain this.

M.: See how though rope and snake are quite different from each other, yet ignorance of the rope makes it appear as a snake; so also the Self being hidden by the darkness of veiling, does not shine forth, and in its place only the functions of the ego, doership, etc., are seen.

29-31. Therefore enquire into the nature of the five sheaths, find them, realize them, and then reject them as non-self. There must be the unchanging witness of changes, originating and destroying these phenomena. Find and realize Him as the Self.

D.: Distinct from all the phenomena, where can the witness be?

M.: There is the triad composed of the knower, knowledge, and the known. Of these, the knower is the subject; knowledge is the intellect; and the known, the objects. This triad arises and flourishes in the waking and dream states and merges in the insentience of the deep sleep state. That which, remaining as the sole unchanging consciousness, illuminates and causes the appearance of all these three states, is the witnessing Self. Discern It and realize It.

32. *D.:* When, according to your instructions, I enquire into the five sheaths and reject them as being non-self, I do not find anything left but simple void. Where then is the Self?

33-35. *M.:* To say that there is nothing left behind the five sheaths, is like saying, "I have no tongue to speak".

D.: How so?

M.: Unless one has a tongue one cannot say that one has no tongue with which to speak. Similarly, unless there is the seer of the void one cannot say there is nothing left. Otherwise one must not say anything. On the contrary since the speaker says that nothing is seen, it is obvious that the Self remains there revealing nothing besides Itself.

D.: If so, how can It remain unknown?

M.: The Self sees all but is seen by none else.

D.: Being self-shining, It can know things without any aids, but there is nothing which can know It. It knows all; It knows that there is nothing; It is the inmost core of all; It remains as the pure, untainted, ether of Consciousness, unseen by anything. It remains impartite. The knower of all, the pure Knowledge, is the Self.

36-43. *D.:* How does the Self remain unknown by anything, yet knowing all?

M.: The sheaths appear as existing. When they are rejected, their absence appears as a blank or nothing. The sheaths, the blank and all else that appears, are but insentient and cannot of their own accord show themselves forth, but must be seen by a seer. In the absence of the seer, nothing can be seen.

D.: How so?

M.: Objects like a pot, etc., manifest only to a seer; otherwise they do not exist. In the same manner, the void beyond the five sheaths manifests because there is the seer. Unless there is the witness, how can the void appear as though nothing were seen? Not being conscious but only insentient, it cannot show itself forth unless the witness sees and recognizes it.

D.: Though insentient it can manifest itself.

M.: In this case let objects like a pot, etc., show themselves forth in the absence of their seer. This is impossible. The void appearing as nothing is also insentient and therefore cannot shine forth by itself. It must be illumined by a light beyond and witnessed by it.

D.: How?

M.: Just as clouds, etc. above, or objects like a pot, etc., below are not self-luminous but must be illumined by the sun which lies millions of miles beyond and is self-effulgent, so also the void, etc. beyond the intellect and objects fancied by it, are insentient and non-luminous, but must be illumined by the transcendent, self-shining Consciousness. Beyond the void and distinct from it, there is the witness seeing the void and all else. He is the Self: unknown by anything, yet knowing all. By your intellect made subtle, find and realize the Self.

44-45. On the nature of the Self being thus made clear by the Master's words, like an apple in one's hand, the disciple was able directly to realize the Self. He then expressed his joy thus: "O Master, I have directly experienced the Self! I have now known It well!"

M.: How do you find the Self to be?

D.: Witness of all objects, void, etc., knowledge aware of all, very majestic, inestimable, unfathomable, beyond the senses, mind, intellect, etc., unassociated, untainted, formless, not gross, not subtle, not atomic, not massive, not white nor black nor otherwise colored, not dark nor bright, but finer and purer than ether, is the Self. Not the least trace of any change is to be found there. Owing to the light of Consciousness, all changing objects and the void appear outside the intellect and far from it; the Self has no modification.

M.: How then do the notions, "I am fat; I am lean," appear in the Self?

D.: The veiling factor of ignorance hides the true nature of the Self from all; without seeing the Self, all mistake the sheaths for the Self. This is owing to ignorance only. In fact there is not the least modification in the Self. Though pure and colorless, the sky seems blue; similarly ignorance makes the Self look as if changing, whereas It remains only unchanging and untainted.

Here and now It is clearly known; It can never be absent. O, is it not a wonder that, though ever so immediate and real, there should have been this great illusion that the Self is not seen! It is like the owl seeing nothing but darkness round it in the dazzling light of the sun! O! The Self is effulgent and manifest! Yet an illusion spreads a darkness over us to make us feel, "The Self is not seen"! Really, it is a wonder! Can there be darkness in midday? Before the ever-bright, ever-manifest supreme Self, can there remain any veiling? Whence can it arise? How can one even think of it? Surely veiling is itself an illusion; it is a mere word; there is no sense in it!

M.: If there is no veiling how did the Self lie hidden so long?

D.: Though unreal, this ignorance flourished on the non-enquiry of the individual. Just as one's non-enquiry hides the rope from view and presents it as a snake, so also non-enquiry into the Self hides It from being seen and this is called the veiling aspect of beginningless ignorance. Now that the Self is realized, the so-called veiling is nowhere to be seen. Lo, the Self is here and now found to be the ever-shining Witness! Wonder of wonders! Like an apple in my hand I have now clearly realized the Self. Now Lord, Master, fortunately by your grace I am blessed; my task is finished!

46-50. On hearing the happy words of the blessed disciple, the Master is pleased and speaks as follows: "Wise, worthy son, by God's grace you have realized what one must realize!

By His grace your ignorance has ended, by which even the learned, unable to realize the Self, remain deluded. Happily you have got what is denied even to great scholars! Jointly all the merits of your past births have this day borne fruit! What can be the excellence of your merits that they have borne this fruit? Blessed are you! Ended is your task! You are an accomplished man! How wonderful that you have gained that which must be gained above all! In order to gain this, all the great works, vows, austerities, worship, *yoga* and other laborious tasks are undertaken; and only to know it, all the trouble and worry of these processes is gone through. All your travail is now over! All the labor of your past births has this day borne fruit! Only in ignorance of this supreme Thing all people lie sunk in the fathomless sea of repeated births and deaths. You have reached the shore beyond this sea. In ignorance of all this , men mistake the body, senses, etc., for the Self. You have found this Self. Therefore you are really wise, truly intelligent. There can be no doubt of this.

So far you have really quested and realized the significance of 'thou' in the text, 'That thou art'. On the same lines pursue your enquiry and realize the significance of 'That' in the text."

51-52. *D.:* Please tell me, Master, the direct and intended meanings of "That", just as for "thou" they are the sheaths and the witness respectively.

M.: The whole universe is composed of the five factors:

"being," "shining," "pleasing," "name" and "form", the five sheaths and the external objects like a pot, etc.

D.: Please explain the five factors of the external objects.

M.: That a pot is, is its "being" aspect; that it appears, is its "shining" aspect; that it is dear to us, is its "pleasing" aspect; "pot" is its "name" aspect; and its shape is its "form" aspect. So it is with all objects. Of the five factors, the first three are characteristic of *Brahman*, and the remaining two, of the world.

The direct meaning of "That" is the world factors, i.e. names and forms; the intended meaning is *Brahman*—the composite of Being-Shining-Pleasing. Just as the beginningless ignorance veils the self-evident difference between the sheaths and their witness, so also it veils the similar difference between the Being-Shining-Pleasing and the name and form factors. Again, as enquiry scatters away the veiling power, the Being-Knowledge-Bliss can be seen distinct from the name and form aspect.

53-54. *D.:* What is the "fruit" of knowing the direct and intended meanings of "That" and "Thou" in the text, "That thou art"?

M.: The text speaks of the sameness of "thou" the witness of the five sheaths, and of "That", i.e., *Brahman* or the Being-Knowledge-Bliss lying beyond the names and forms in the universe. These are the intended meanings of "thou" and "That". There can be no identity between the five sheaths of the individual, the direct meaning of "thou", and the names and forms in the universe, the direct meaning of "That". Hence, it follows that the five sheaths and the names and forms are only illusory. To know the witness and *Brahman* to be one is the "fruit" of knowledge.

D.: How can these be one and the same?

M.: Being only Being-Knowledge-Bliss, both of them must be the same. Just as the ether in a pot and that in the open have the same characteristics and are therefore identical, so also the witness and *Brahman* having the same characteristics, namely Being, Knowledge and Bliss, are one and the same. The ether of the pot is that of the open and *vice versa*; so also the witness is *Brahman*, and *Brahman* is the witness.

55-56. Inasmuch as *Brahman* is impartite perfect wholeness, the witness being *Brahman* must also be impartite, perfect wholeness. Therefore it is established that the Self is one unbroken bliss.

D.: What is the "fruit" of this knowledge?

M.: To reject the five sheaths and names and forms of objects as something inexpressible, only superimposed on the Reality, and illusory; to practice that the substratum, i.e., the *Brahman* of Being-Knowledge-Bliss is the Self; and to realize It as "I am Brahman" with the resulting supreme bliss of being *Brahman*, is the "fruit" of this knowledge. Here ends the chapter on reflection.

57. The wise student who carefully reads and practices it can realize himself as *Brahman*, i.e., Being-Knowledge-Bliss.

Chapter VI

Vâsanâkshaya

The Annihilation of Latencies

1. This chapter succeeds the five earlier ones on super-imposition, its withdrawal, the requisites of the seeker, hearing, and reflection. To the disciple who, after reflecting on the Self, has gained direct knowledge, the Master further says as follows:

2. "Wise son, the *shâstras* have nothing more to teach you; you have finished with them. Henceforth you must meditate on the Self. The Scriptures say: 'Dear! The Self must be heard of, reflected and meditated upon'. Having finished reflection, you must proceed with meditation. Now give up the *shâstras.*"

D.: Is it proper to give them up?

M.: Yes, it is proper. Now that, by enquiry, you have known what needs to be known, you can unhesitatingly give them up.

D.: But the *shâstras* say that to the last moment of death, one should not give them up.

M.: Their purpose is to teach the truth. After it is gained, of what further use can they be? A further study will be so much waste of time and labour. Therefore leave them aside. Take to unbroken meditation.

D.: Is this statement supported by scriptures?

M.: Yes.

D.: How?

M.: They say: After repeatedly hearing from the Master about the Self, reflecting on It, and directly knowing it, the seeker should give up the *shâstras* even as the pole used to stir up the corpse in the burning ground is finally consigned to the burning fire of the corpse. From a study of the *shâstras* let the seeker of liberation gather an indirect knowledge of the Self and put it into practice by reflecting on It until, by experiencing

77

It, a direct knowledge is gained. Later, like a gatherer of grains who takes the grains and rejects the chaff, let him leave the *shâstras* aside. The man desirous of liberation should make use of *shâstras* only to gain knowledge of the Self and then proceed to reflect on It; he should not be simply talking *Vedânta*, nor even be thinking of it. For talk results only in so much strain on speech; and it is similar with thinking, on the mind; no useful purpose can be served by either. Therefore, know only what need be known and give up tiresome study. Controlling his speech and mind, a sensible seeker should always engage in meditation. This is the teaching of the *shâstras*.

7. Wise son, now that you have known what need be known from them, you should efface the impressions left by your studies.

D.: What constitutes these impressions?

M.: It is the inclination of the mind always to study *Vedântic* literature, to understand the meanings of the texts, to commit them to memory and constantly be thinking of them. Since this inclination obstructs meditation, a wise man must overcome it with every effort. Next, the latencies connected with the world *(lokavâsanâ)* must be eliminated.

8. *D.:* What are these latencies?

M.: To think: "this is my country," "this is my family pedigree," and "this is the tradition." Should any one praise or censure any of these, the reactions of the mind denote the latencies connected with the world. Give them up. Later on, give up the latencies connected with the body also *(dehavâsanâ)*.

9-13. *D.:* What are they?

M.: To think oneself to be of such and such an age, young or old, and desire the full span of life with health, strength and good looks. Generally, thoughts pertaining to the body indicate these latencies. Ambition in the world and love of the body distract the mind and prevent meditation on *Brahman*. Since all objects are ephemeral, they must be eschewed. Then the latencies connected with enjoyments *(bhogavâsanâ)* must be given up.

D.: What are these?

M.: These are made up of thoughts like: "this is good and I must have it," "this is not so and let it leave me," "now I have gained so much and let me gain more," and so on.

D.: How can this be overcome?

M.: This can be overcome by looking with disgust upon all enjoyments as on vomit or excreta and developing dispassion for them. Dispassion is the only remedy for this mad craving. After this, the mind must be cleared of the six passions, namely, lust, anger, greed, delusion, pride and jealousy.

D.: How can this be done?

M.: By friendship with the holy (*maitrî*), compassion for the afflicted (*karunâ*), rejoicing in the joy of the virtuous (*mudîtâ*) and being indifferent to the shortcomings of the sinful (*upeksha*).

Next, the latencies connected with the objects of the senses *(vishayavâsanâ)* such as sound, etc., must be restrained. These latencies are the running of the senses, such as hearing, etc., after their objects.

D.: How can these latencies be restrained?

M.: By a practice of the six-fold discipline consisting of *shama, dama, uparati, titikshâ, samâdhâna* and *shraddhâ*, i.e., withdrawing the mind from going outwards, controlling the senses, not thinking of the objects of the senses, forbearance, fixing the mind on the Real and faith.

Next, all latencies connected with mutual attachments must be overcome.

14-15. *D.:* What are they?

M.: Though the senses are restrained, yet the mind always thinks of objects: "there is that," "there is this," "it is such and such," "it is this way," or "otherwise,'" and so on. Because of brooding over objects, the mind becomes attached to them. This constant brooding is referred to as the latencies connected with mental attachment.

D.: How can this be checked?

M.: By practicing *uparati*, which means desisting from all thoughts, after concluding by proper reasoning that they are only fruitless daydreams.

16. When, in the correct manner, all this has been accomplished, the greatest evil-doer, namely the latency connected with wrong identity (viparîta vâsanâ), must be put to an end, even with

great effort.

17. *D.:* What is this latency connected with wrong identity?

M.: Owing to beginningless ignorance the non-self is mistaken for the Self as "I am the body." From time immemorial, this ignorance has been hardy and can only be ended by the practice of *Brahman.*

18-20. *D.:* What is this practice?

M.: It consists in discarding the body, senses, etc., as being non-self, and always remembering that "I am *Brahman,*" and remaining as consciousness, witnessing the insentient sheaths. Meditating on *Brahman* in solitude; speaking of or teaching only *Brahman* in the company of others; not to speak or think of anything but It, always one-pointedly to think of *Brahman,* is the practice.

"So say the wise. By this, transcend the ego and then proceed to eliminate the idea of 'mine'". (*Yoga* Vasishtha)

21-22. *D.:* What is the nature of this idea?

M.: It consists in the single concept of "mine" in relation to the body or whatever pertains to it, such as name, form, clothing, caste, conduct or professions of life.

D.: How does this go away?

M.: By a steadfast meditation on the Real.

D.: How?

M.: Always to be aware that the body, etc., its interest and effects, enjoyments, activities etc., are only figments of ignorance on pure knowledge i.e., the Self; that like the appearance of silver on nacre, ornaments in gold, water in mirage, blueness in the sky, or waves in water, all are only false representations or illusory modes of the Self. In reality there is nothing but ourselves. Next the sense of differentiation *(bheda vâsanâ)* must go.

23-25. *D.:* What is this sense of differentiation?

M.: It consists in ideas like: "I am the witness of this," "all that is seen is only insentient and illusory," "here is the world," "these are the individuals,"; "this one is the disciple and the other, the Master,"; "this is *Îshvara,*" and so on. This must go by a practice of non-duality.

This practice is to remain non-dual Being-Knowledge-Bliss, untainted and free from thoughts of reality or unreality, ignorance or its illusory effects, and internal or external differentiation. This is accomplished by a constant practice of modeless *(nirvikalpa) samâdhi.* Here remains the experience of *Brahman* only.

After leaving the sense of differentiation far behind, the attachment to non-duality must later be given up.

26.-27. *D.:* How is this to be done?

M.: Even this state must finally pass into untellable and unthinkable Reality absolutely free from modes and even non-duality. The bliss of liberation is only this and nothing more. When the mind is cleared of all latent impurities, it remains untainted, crystal-clear so that it cannot be said to exist or not to exist and it becomes one with the Real, transcending speech and thought. This unmoded, untainted fixity of the mind is known as realization or liberation while alive.

28. Though direct knowledge of the Self has been gained, yet until this realization ensues, to be liberated while alive, one should always meditate on *Brahman* with proper control of mind and senses.

Thus ends this chapter.

Chapter VII

Sâksâtkâra

Realization

1. In the foregoing chapters, it was said that direct knowledge must first be gained and then the latent tendencies of the mind wiped out so that *Brahman* may be realized. Now realization is dealt with.

The Master says: "Wise son, now that you have gained direct knowledge by enquiry into the Self, you should proceed with meditation."

2. *D.:* Master, now that I have gained direct knowledge by enquiry and my task is finished why should I meditate further and to what end?

3-4. *M.:* Though by reflection, direct knowledge of the Self has been gained, *Brahman* cannot be realized without meditation. In order to experience, "I am *Brahman*," you must practice meditation.

5-6. *D.:* You ask me to pursue meditation for realizing *Brahman?* I have already gained direct knowledge by enquiry into the sacred text. Why should I now practice meditation?

M.: If you mean to say that enquiry into the sacred text results in realizing *Brahman*, who can deny it? No one. Truly this enquiry must end in the realization of *Brahman*.

Let us now enquire into the meaning of the text. Whose identity with whom is implied in it? It must be the identity of the consciousness witnessing the five sheaths of the individual, the implied meaning of "thou", with *Brahman*, the implied meaning of "That"; it cannot be of the *jîva*, i.e., the personal soul with *Brahman*. By enquiry the identity of the witnessing consciousness with *Brahman* has certainly been found. Of what use can this identity of the witness with *Brahman* be to you?

7. *D.:* On enquiry into the meaning of the sacred text, when one has realized that the witness is *Brahman* and *vice versa*, how can you raise the question, "Of what use can it be to the person?" Its use is evident. Formerly the seeker was ignorant of the identity and now by enquiry he is aware of it.

M.: By enquiry you have certainly known that the witness is *Brahman* and that the unbroken, all-perfect *Brahman* is the witness. Still this knowledge is not the end and cannot serve your purpose. Suppose a poor beggar, who was ignorant of the fact that a king resident in a fort was the emperor of the world, later knew it. How does this newly acquired knowledge improve his position? It cannot serve any useful purpose for him.

8. *D.:* Before enquiry, ignorance prevails. After enquiry, knowledge is gained that the witness is *Brahman*. Now knowledge has taken the place of ignorance. This is the use.

M.: How does this affect the fact? Whether you have known it or not, the witness ever remains *Brahman*. Your knowledge of the fact has not made *Brahman* of the witness. Whether the poor beggar knew it or not, the king in the fort was the emperor. His knowledge did not make an emperor of the king in the fort. Now that you have known the witness to be *Brahman*, what has happened to you? Tell me. There can be no change in you.

9. *D.:* Why not? There is a difference. The sacred text teaches, "That thou art". On enquiring into its significance I have found that the witness of the five sheaths in me is the same as *Brahman*. From this I have known that I am *Brahman*, which forms another sacred text. To me who was ignorant of the witness being the same as *Brahman*, this knowledge has dawned, with the result that I have realized *Brahman*.

M.: How can you claim to have realized *Brahman*? If by the text "I am Brahman" you understand yourself to be *Brahman*, who is this "I" but the *jîva*, the personal soul or the ego? How can the ego be *Brahman*? Just as with his knowledge of the king, the beggar cannot himself be the king, so also the changeful ego can never be identical with the changeless *Brahman*.

10-14. *D.:* Certainly so. But on enquiring, "Who am I?" it becomes plain that by non-enquiry the unchanging witness had mistaken the changing ego for himself. Now he knows, "I am not the changing ego but remain its unchanging conscious witness". Now, it is but right that the witness should say, "I am *Brahman*". What can be discordant in this?

M.: How can you hold that the witness says, "I am *Brahman*"? Does the unchanging witness or the changing ego say it? If you say that it is the witness, you are wrong. For the witness remains unchanging as the witness of the I-conceit. He is not the conceit itself. Otherwise he cannot have the quality of being the witness for he will himself be changing. Being unchanging the witness is free from the least trace of any notion such as "I" or *Brahman* and cannot therefore know "I am *Brahman*". There is no ground for your contention that the witness says so.

D.: Then who knows, "I am *Brahman*"?

M.: From what has been said before, it must follow that the individual soul, the *jîva,* or the I-conceit, must have this knowledge.

D.: How does this follow?

M.: In order to be free from the repeated cycle of births and deaths, the ignorant man is obliged to practice the knowledge "I am *Brahman*". There is no ignorance for the witness. When there is no ignorance, there can be no knowledge either. Only the ignorant must seek knowledge. Who but the I-conceit can be the subject of ignorance or of knowledge? It is self-evident that the witnessing Self, being the substratum on which knowledge or ignorance appears, must itself be free from them. On the contrary the I-conceit is known to possess knowledge or ignorance. For ask him, "Do you know the Self witnessing you?" and he will answer, "Who is that witness? I do not know him". Here the ignorance of the I-conceit is obvious.

On hearing from the *Vedânta* that there is an inner witness to him, he indirectly knows that the Self is his witness. Then, enquiring into the Self, the evil of ignorance that It does not shine forth is drawn off and directly he knows the witnessing Self. Here again the knowledge of the I-conceit is also clear.

It is only the *jîva* and not the witness who has the knowledge or ignorance that there is, or is not, the inner witness. You must now admit that the *jîva* has the knowledge that, "I am *Brahman*". Now, for the reason that the changing *jîva* has become aware of the unchanging witness, he cannot be the same as the witness. Because he had seen him, the poor beggar cannot be the king. So also the changing *jîva* cannot be the witness. Without being the witnessing Self, the changing entity cannot be Brahman. So this experience, "I am *Brahman*" is impossible.

15. *D.:* How can you say that merely seeing the witness, I cannot know that I am the witness? Ignorant of his true being as the substratum or the witnessing Consciousness, the *jîva* moves about as the I-conceit. However, on a careful enquiry into his true nature he knows the witness and identifies himself as the witness who is well known to be the unbroken, all perfect *Brahman*. Thus the experience, "I am *Brahman*," is real.

M.: What you say is true provided that the *jîva* can identify himself as the witness. The witness is undoubtedly *Brahman*. But how can the mere sight of the witness help the *jîva* merge himself into the witness? Unless the *jîva* remains the witness, he cannot know himself as the witness. Merely by seeing the king, a poor beggar cannot know himself to be the king. But when he becomes the king, he can know himself as the king. Similarly the *jîva*, remaining changeful and without becoming the unchanging witness, cannot know himself as the witness. If he cannot be the witness, how can he be the unbroken, all-perfect *Brahman*? He cannot be. Just as at the sight of the king in a fort, a poor beggar cannot become king and much less sovereign of the universe, so also only at the sight of the witness, who is much finer than ether and free from triads, such as the knower, knowledge and the known, eternal, pure, aware, free, real, supreme and blissful, the *jîva* cannot become the witness, much less the unbroken, all-perfect *Brahman*, and cannot know, "I am *Brahman*".

16. *D.:* If so, how is it that the two words of the same case-ending (*samânâdhikarana*)—"I" and "*Brahman*"—are placed in apposition in the sacred text "I am *Brahman*"? According to grammatical rules the *shruti* clearly proclaims the same rank to the *jîva* and *Brahman*. How is this to be explained?

17-18. *M.:* The common agreement between two words in apposition is of two kinds: *mukhya* and *bâdha*, i.e., unconditional and conditional. Here the *shruti* does not convey the unconditional meaning.

D.: What is this unconditional meaning?

M.: The ether in a jar has the same characteristics as that in another jar, or in a room, or in the open. Therefore the one ether is the same as the other. Similarly with air, fire, water, earth, sunlight, etc. Again the god in one image is the same as that in another and the witnessing consciousness in one being is the same as that in another. The *shruti* does not mean this kind of identity between the *jîva* and *Brahman*, but means the other, the conditional meaning.

D.: What is it?

M.: Discarding all appearances, the sameness of the substratum in all.

Please explain this.

M.: "I am *Brahman*" means that, after discarding the I-conceit, only the residual being or the pure consciousness that is left over can be *Brahman*. It is absurd to say that, without discarding but retaining the individuality, the *jîva*, on seeing *Brahman* but not becoming *Brahman*, can know himself as *Brahman*. A poor beggar must first cease to be a beggar and obtain rule over a state in order to know himself as king; a man desirous of godhood first drowns himself in the Ganges and leaving this body, becomes himself a celestial being; by his extraordinary one-pointed devotion a devotee leaves off his body and merges into god, before he can know himself to be god. In all these cases when the beggar knows himself to be king, or the man to be a celestial being, or the devotee to be god, they cannot retain their former individualities and also identify themselves as the superior beings. In the same way, the seeker of liberation must first cease to be an individual before he can rightly say, "I am *Brahman*". This is the significance of the sacred text. Without completely losing one's individuality one cannot be *Brahman*. Therefore to realize *Brahman*, the loss of the individuality is a *sine qua non*.

D.: The changeful individual soul cannot be *Brahman*. Even though he rids himself of the individuality, how can he become *Brahman*?

19. *M.:* Just as a maggot, losing its nature, becomes a wasp. A

maggot is brought by a wasp and kept in its hive. From time to time the wasp visits the hive and stings the maggot so that it always remains in dread of its tormentor. The constant thought of the wasp transforms the maggot into a wasp. Similarly, constantly meditating on *Brahman*, the seeker loses his original nature and becomes himself *Brahman*. This is the realization of *Brahman*.

20. *D.:* This cannot illustrate the point, for the *jîva* is changing and falsely presented on the pure Being, *Brahman*, which is the Real. When a false thing has lost its falsity, the whole entity is gone; how can it become the Real?

21. *M.:* Your doubt, how a superimposed falsity turns out to be its substratum, the Real, is easily cleared. See how the nacre-silver ceases to be silver and remains as nacre, or a rope-snake ceasing to be snake remains over as rope. Similarly, with the *jîva* superimposed on the Reality, *Brahman*.

D.: These are illusions which are not conditioned *(nirupâdhika bhrama)* whereas the appearance of the *jîva* is conditioned *(sopadhika bhrama)* and appears as superimposed only on the internal faculty, the mind. So long as there is the mind, there will also be the *jîva* or the individual, and the mind is the result of past *karma*. As long as this remains unexhausted, the *jîva* must also be present. Just as the reflection of one's face is contingent upon the mirror or water in front, so is individuality, on the mind, the effect of one's past *karma*. How can this individuality be done away with?

M.: Undoubtedly, individuality lasts as long as the mind exists. Just as the reflected image disappears with the removal of the mirror in front, so also individuality can he effaced by stilling the mind by meditation.

D.: The individuality being thus lost, the *jîva* becomes void. Having become void, how can he become *Brahman*?

M.: The *jîva* is only a false appearance not apart from its substratum; it is conditional on ignorance, or the mind, on whose removal it is left as the substratum, as in the case of a dream-person.

22-23. *D.:* How?

M.: The waking man functions as the dreamer *(taijasa)* in his dreams. The dreamer is neither identical with, nor separate from, the waking man *(vishva)*. For the man sleeping happily on his bed has not moved out, whereas as the dreamer he had wandered about in other places, busy with many things. The wanderer of the dream cannot be the man resting in his bed. Can he then be different? Not so either. For on waking from sleep, he says, "In my dream I went to so many places, did so many things and was happy or otherwise". Clearly he identifies himself with the experiencer of the dream. Moreover no other experiencer can be seen.

D.: Not different from, nor identical with, the waking experiencer, who is this dream-experiencer?

M.: Being a creation of the illusory power of sleep the dream-experiencer is only an illusion like the snake on a rope. With the finish of the illusory power of dream, the dreamer vanishes only to wake up as the real substratum, the original individual self of the waking state. Similarly the empirical self, the *jîva*, is neither the unchanging *Brahman* nor other than It. In the internal faculty, the mind, fancied by ignorance, the Self is reflected and the reflection presents itself as the empirical, changing and individual self. This is a superimposed false appearance. Since the superimposition cannot remain apart from its substratum, this empirical self cannot be other than the absolute Self.

D.: Who is this?

M.: Successively appearing in the ignorance-created mind and disappearing in deep sleep, swoon etc., this empirical self is inferred to be only a phantom. Simultaneously with the disappearance of the medium or the limiting adjunct *(upâdhi)*, the mind, the *jîva* becomes the substratum, the true Being or *Brahman*. Destroying the mind, the *jîva* can know itself as *Brahman*.

24. *D.:* With the destruction of the limiting adjunct, the *jîva* being lost, how can he say "I am *Brahman*"?

M.: When the limiting ignorance of dream vanishes, the dreamer is not lost, but emerges as the waking experiencer. So also when the mind is lost, the *jîva* emerges as his true Being— *Brahman*. Therefore, as soon as the mind is annihilated leaving no trace behind, the *jîva* will surely realize, "I am the Being-

Knowledge-Bliss, non-dual *Brahman*; *Brahman* is I, the Self."

D.: In that case the state must be modeless like that of deep sleep. How can there be the experience, "I am *Brahman*"?

M.: Just as at the end of a dream, the dreamer rising up as the waking experiencer says, "All along I was dreaming that I wandered in strange places, etc., but I am only lying down on the bed"; or a madman cured of his madness remains pleased with himself; or a patient cured of his illness wonders at his past sufferings; or a poor man on becoming a king, forgets or laughs at his penurious state; or a man on becoming a celestial being enjoys the new bliss; or a devotee on uniting with the Lord of his devotion remains blissful, so also the *jîva* on emerging as *Brahman* wonders how all along being only *Brahman* he was moving about as a helpless being imagining a world, god and individuals, and asks himself what became of all those fancies and how, remaining all alone as Being-Knowledge-Bliss, free from any differentiation, internal or external, he now certainly experiences the supreme bliss of *Brahman*. Thus, realization is possible for the *jîva* only on the complete destruction of the mind and not otherwise.

25. *D.:* Experience can be of the mind only. When it is destroyed, who can have the experience, "I am *Brahman*"?

M.: You are right. The destruction of the mind is of two kinds: *rûpa* and *arûpa*, i.e., in its form-aspect and in its formless aspect. All this while, I have been speaking of destroying the former mind. Only when it ceases to be in its formless aspect, will experience be impossible, as you say.

D.: Please explain these two forms of the mind and their destruction.

M.: The latent impression *(vâsanâs)* manifesting as modes *(vrittis)* constitute the form-aspect of the mind. Their effacement is the destruction of this aspect of mind. On the other hand, upon the perishing of the latencies, the supervening state of *samâdhi* in which there is no stupor of sleep, no vision of the world, but only the unmoded Being-Knowledge-Bliss, is the formless aspect of mind. The loss of this amounts to the loss of the formless aspect of mind. Should this also be lost, there can be no experience—not even of the realization of supreme Bliss.

D.: When does this destruction take place?

M.: On the disembodiment of the liberated being. It cannot happen so long as he is alive in the body. The mind is lost in its form-aspect but not in its formless one of *Brahman*. Hence the experience of bliss for the sage, liberated while alive.

26-27. *D.:* In brief, what is realization?

M.: To destroy the mind in its form-aspect, functioning as the limiting adjunct to the individual; to recover the pure mind in its formless aspect whose nature is only Being-Knowledge-Bliss; and to experience "I am *Brahman*" is realization.

D.: Is this view supported by others as well?

M.: Yes. Shri Shankarâchârya has said: "Just as in the ignorant state, unmindful of the identity of the Self with *Brahman*, one truly believes oneself to be the body, so also after knowledge, to be free from the illusion of the body, being the Self, and becoming unaware of the body, undoubtingly and unmistakably always to experience the Self as Being-Knowledge-Bliss, identical with *Brahman*, is called realization".

28. To be fixed as the real Self is realization, say the sages.

D.: Who says it and where?

29. *M.:* Vasishtha has said in *Yoga* Vasishtha: "Just as the mind in a stone remains quiet and modeless, so also, like the interior of the stone, to remain unmoded and thought-free, but not in slumber nor aware of duality, is to be fixed as the real Self."

30-31. Therefore, without effacing the form-aspect of the mind and remaining fixed as the true Self, how can anyone realize "I am *Brahman*"? It cannot be. Briefly put, one should still the mind to destroy one's individuality and thus remain fixed as the real Self of Being-Knowledge-Bliss so that, in accordance with the text "I am *Brahman*", one can realize *Brahman*. On the other hand, on the strength of the direct knowledge of *Brahman*, to say, "I am *Brahman*" is as silly as a poor beggar upon seeing the king declaring himself to be the king. Not to claim by words but to be fixed as the real Self and know, "I am *Brahman*' is realization of *Brahman*.

32. *D.:* How will the sage be who has undoubtingly, unmistakably and steadily realized *Brahman*?

M.: Always remaining as Being-Knowledge-Bliss, non-dual,

all-perfect, all-alone, unitary *Brahman,* he will be unshaken even while experiencing the results of past *karma* now in fruition. *(prârabdha).*

33-35. *D.:* Being only *Brahman,* how can he be subject to the experiences and activities resulting from past *karma?*

M.: For the sage undoubtingly and unmistakably fixed as the real Self, there can remain no past *karma.* In its absence there can be no fruition; consequently no experience nor any activity. Being only unmoded *Brahman,* there can be no experiencer, no experiences and no objects of experience. Therefore no past *karma* can be said to remain for him.

D.: Why should we not say that his past *karma* is now working itself out?

M.: Who is the questioner? He must be a deluded being and not a sage.

D.: Why?

M.: Experience implies delusion; without the one, the other cannot be. Unless there is an object, no experience is possible. All objective knowledge is delusion. There is no duality in *Brahman.* Certainly, all names and forms are by ignorance superimposed on *Brahman.* Therefore the experiencer must be ignorant only and not a sage. Having already enquired into the nature of things and known them to be illusory names and forms born of ignorance, the sage remains fixed as *Brahman* and knows all to be only *Brahman.* Who is to enjoy what? No one and nothing. Therefore there is no past *karma* left nor present enjoyments nor any activity for the wise one.

36-37. *D.:* However, we do not see him free from the experience of past *karma;* on the other hand he goes through them like an ordinary ignorant man. How is this to be explained?

M.: In his view there is nothing like past *karma,* enjoyments or activities.

D.: What is his view?

M.: For him there is nothing but the pure, untainted, ether of absolute Knowledge.

D.: But how is he seen to pass through experiences?

M.: Only the others see him so. He is not aware of it.

38-39. *D.:* Is this view confirmed by other authorities?

M.: In *Viveka Chûdâmani,* Shri Achârya has said:

"Simultaneous with the dawn of knowledge, ignorance with all its effects flees away from the sage and so he cannot be an enjoyer. However, the ignorant wonder how the sage continues to live in the body and act like others. From the ignorant point of view, the scriptures have admitted the momentum of past *karma,* but not from the point of view of the sage himself."

40. *D.:* If truly he is no enjoyer, why should he appear to others to be so?

M.: Owing to their ignorance, the others regard him as an enjoyer.

41-43. *D.:* Can this be so?

M.: Yes. To the ignorant only, the non-dual, pure ether of absolute Knowledge manifests Itself as various beings, the world, God, different names and forms, I, you, he, it, this and that. Like the illusion of a man on a post, silver on nacre, snake on rope, utensils in clay, or ornaments in gold, different names and forms on the ether of Knowledge delude the ignorant. The sage, who by practice of knowledge has destroyed ignorance and gained true knowledge, will always remain only as the ether of absolute Knowledge, unaware of enjoyments of fruits of actions or of worldly activities. Being That, he can be aware as the ether of Knowledge only. Nevertheless, owing to their ignorance, others see him otherwise, i.e., as an embodied being acting like themselves. But he remains only pure, untainted ether, without any activity.

44-46. *D.:* Can it be illustrated how the sage, remaining himself inactive, appears active to others?

M.: Two friends sleep side by side. One of them reposes in dreamless sleep whereas the other dreams that he is wandering about with his friend. Though in complete repose, this man appears active to the dreamer. Similarly, although the sage remains inactive as the blissful ether of absolute Knowledge, he appears to be active to those who in ignorance remain always caught up in names and forms. It must now be clear that the realized sage, being the pure Self, is not involved in action but only appears to be so.

47-48. *D.:* Not that there are no experiences whatever for the realized sage, but they are only illusory. For Knowledge can destroy the *karma* already stored and the future *karma* (*sanchita* and *agâmî*) but not the *karma* which having already begun to bear fruit (*prârabdha*) must exhaust itself. As long as it is there, even from his own point of view, activities will persist, though illusorily.

M.: This cannot be. In which state do these three kinds of *karma* exist—knowledge or ignorance? Owing to delusion, it must be said, they are operative only in ignorance. But in knowledge, there being no delusion, there is no *prârabdha*. Always remaining undeluded as the transcendental Self, how can the delusion of the fruition of *karma* occur to one? Can the delusion of dream-experience return to him who has awakened from it? To the sage free from illusion there can be no experience of *karma*. He ever remains unaware of the world but aware of the Self as the non-dual, unbroken, unitary, solid, unmoded ether of absolute Knowledge, and of nothing besides.

49. *D.:* The *Upanishad* admits past *karma* in the text, "As long as his past *karma* is not exhausted the sage cannot be disembodied, and there will be illusory activities for him".

M.: You are not right. The activities and experiences of the fruits of action and the world seem illusory to the practitioner of Knowledge and they completely vanish to the accomplished sage. The practitioner practices as follows:

"I am the witness; the objects and activities are seen by, and known to, me. I remain conscious and these are insentient. Only *Brahman* is real; all else is unreal". The practice ends with the realization that all these are insentient, consisting of names and forms and cannot exist in the past, present or future; therefore they vanish. There being nothing to witness, witnessing ends by merging into *Brahman*. Only the Self is now left over as *Brahman*. For the sage aware of the Self only, there can remain only *Brahman* and no thought of *karma*, or worldly activities.

D.: Why then does the *shruti* mention past *karma* in this connection?

M.: It does not refer to the accomplished sage.

D.: Whom does it refer to?

M.: Only to the ignorant.

D.: Why?

M.: Although from his own point of view, the sage has no enjoyment of the fruits of actions, yet the ignorant are deluded on seeing his activities. Even if told there is no enjoyment for him, the ignorant will not accept it but continue to doubt how the sage remains active. To remove such doubt, the *shruti* says to the ignorant that *prârabdha* still remains for the sage. But it does not say to the sage, "You have *prârabdha*". Therefore the *shruti* which speaks of residual *prârabdha* for the sage, really does not speak of it from his point of view.

50-51. *D.:* Realization can result only after complete annihilation of individuality. But who will agree to sacrifice his individuality?

M.: Being eager to cross over the ocean of the misery of repeated births and deaths and realize the pure, eternal *Brahman,* one will readily sacrifice one's individuality. Just as the man desirous of becoming a celestial being willingly consigns himself to the fire or the Ganges in order to end this human life and emerge as a god, so also the seeker of liberation will, by practice of *shravana, manana,* and *nididhyâsana,* (i.e., hearing, reflection and meditation), sacrifice his individuality to become the supreme *Brahman.*

52. Here ends the chapter on realization.

Diligently studying and understanding this, the seeker will kill the mind which is the limiting adjunct that causes individuality to manifest, and ever live as *Brahman* only.

Chapter VIII

Manonasha

The Extinction of the Mind

1. In the previous chapter, having taught the realization of the non-dual *Brahman*, the Master explains how the extinction of the mind is the sole means of realising *Brahman*.

M.: Wise son, leave off the mind which is a limiting adjunct giving rise to individuality, thus causing that great malady of repeated births and deaths, and realize *Brahman*,

2. *D.:* Master, how can the mind be extinguished? Is it not very hard to do so? Is not the mind very powerful, restive and ever vascillating? How can one relinquish the mind?

3-4. *M.:* To give up the mind is very easy, as easy as crushing a delicate flower, or removing a hair from butter or winking your eyes. Doubt it not. For a self-possessed, resolute seeker not bewitched by the senses, but by strong dispassion grown indifferent to external objects, there cannot be the least difficulty in giving up the mind.

D.: How is it so easy?

M.: The question of difficulty arises only if there is a mind to leave off. Truly speaking, there is no mind. When told, "There is a ghost here,' an ignorant child is deluded into believing the existence of the non-existent ghost and is subject to fear, misery and troubles. Similarly, in the untainted *Brahman*, by fancying things that are not, as this and that, a false entity known as the mind arises, seemingly real, functioning as this and that, and proving uncontrollable and mighty to the unwary; whereas to the self-possessed, discerning seeker who knows its nature, it is easy to relinquish. Only a fool ignorant of its nature says it is most difficult.

5-10. *D.:* What is the nature of mind?

M.: To think this and that. In the absence of thought, there can be no mind. Upon the thoughts being extinguished, the mind will remain only in name like the horn of a hare; it will vanish as a non-entity like a barren woman's son, or a hare's horn, or a flower in the sky. This is also mentioned in the *Yoga* Vasishtha.

D.: How?

M.: Vasishtha says: "Listen, O Râma, there is nothing to speak of as mind. Just as the ether exists without form, so also the mind exists as the blank insentience. It remains only in name; it has no form. It is not outside, nor is it in the heart. Yet like the ether, the mind, though formless, fills all".

D.: How can this be?

M.: Wherever thought arises as this and that, there is the mind.

D.: If there be mind wherever there is thought, are thought and mind different?

M.: Thought is the index of the mind. When a thought arises mind is inferred. In the absence of thought, there can be no mind. Therefore mind is nothing but thought. Thought is itself mind.

D.: What is thought?

M.: Thought is imagination. The thought-free state is Bliss supreme *(Shivasvarûpa)*. Thoughts are of two kinds: the recalling of things experienced, and unexperienced.

11. *D.:* To begin with, please tell me what is thought?.

M.: Sages say that it is nothing but to think of an external object as "this" or "that', 'is' or "is not", "like this" or "like that", etc.

12-13. *D.:* How is this to be classified under the heads of things experienced and unexperienced?

M.: Of objects of senses, such as sound, already experienced as "I saw," "I heard," "I touched", etc.,. and to think of them as having been seen, heard, touched is the recollection of things already experienced. To call to mind unexperienced objects of senses is the thought of unexperienced things.

14. *D.:* That thoughts pertain to things already experienced is understandable. But how to think of those not so experienced

unless they are reminiscences of things already experienced? One can never think of things not experienced. How then can we say that to think of things not already experienced is "thought"?

15. *M.:* Yes, it is quite possible. To think of things not experienced is also thought. Objects unexperienced appear as such only after thinking.

D.: How can the things not already experienced come within the orbit of thought?

M.: By the process of positive and negative induction *(anvaya vyatireka)*, all mental imagery must be said to be thought-forms, whether already experienced or not.

16-17. *D.:* How do you apply the positive and negative induction here?

M.: Whether existent or non-existent, already experienced, or not so experienced, whatever and however something is thought of, it is apprehended. The mere thought of it amounts to apprehension. This is positive induction.

Real or unreal, experienced or not, however it may be, whatever is not thought of, is not apprehended. This is negative induction. From this process also it follows that thought is apprehension.

18. *D.:* How can mere thought of anything be its apprehension also? Things are apprehended directly by the senses or by recall of past experiences to the mind. On the other hand, things unheard of or unseen cannot be apprehended by simply thinking of them. Therefore the logical conclusion that mere thought of anything is its apprehension, does not hold.

M.: You are not right. How can you say that things not directly cognized by the senses are not apprehended? The pleasures of heaven, though not already enjoyed, are vividly pictured in our minds. This is owing to our knowledge of the *shâstras* which depict them. Though not experienced they appear to us as delights not experienced.

19-21 *D.:* Things experienced can be thought of and cognized. But things unexperienced cannot be cognized even if thought of.

M.: Now listen. Experienced or unexperienced things can be cognized. As things already experienced at a distant place are thought of and cognized, so also things unexperienced can be thought of and cognized, on hearing from others, such as the Mt. Meru of bright gold.

Though eyes and ears are closed, yet visions and sounds can be thought of and cognized. Though in dark, one can still think of an object and cognize it. Even without eyes and ears, the blind and the deaf cognize forms and sounds on thinking of them. Therefore, whether already known or unknown, all that is thought of can be apprehended. This is the affirmative proposition.

22. *D.:* What is negation?

M.: In the absence of mind, in swoons, deep sleep or trance there is no thinking and consequently nothing is seen. Not only in these states but also in waking: if one does not think, there is no phenomenon.

23-24. *D.:* Even in waking it cannot be so. Objects of direct cognition, even if not thought of, are apprehended.

M.: No. What you say is not true. Everyday experience teaches us otherwise.

D.: How?

M.: When a man is keenly attentive to something, he does not answer when someone calls. Later he says, "I was intent on something else; I could not hear; I could not see; I was not aware", etc. It is therefore clear that without attention objects of direct cognition cannot be apprehended.

26-28. *D.:* Cannot the objects of direct cognition be apprehended, without attention?

M.: Even though in direct contact with the senses, objects cannot be cognized without attention to them. Though the necklace is in contact with the body, because the wearer is not attentive, its presence is not known. Being unaware of it, she even misses the ornament and searches for it. Though in touch with the body of the wearer the necklace is missed for want of attention.

Again, a patient writhing with pain can be made to forget it by drawing his attention to something else; similarly the grief of bereavement is forgotten by attention being directed to other matters of interest.

It is obvious that without attention, even the objects of direct cognition cannot be recognized.

29-31. From this it follows that the cognition of anything, experienced or not, however it may be, can only be of the form of thought. Therefore, the perception of things has been signified by various terms in *Vedânta,* such as: cognition as this and that, will, thought, mode of mind, intellect, latency, reflected consciousness, the heart-knot, the seen, illusion, the individual, the world, the all, God, etc.

D.: Where has it been said that this knowledge is the all? On the other hand it is said that *Mâyâ* became the all.

M.: Yes. *Mâyâ* is the knowledge which is spoken of. Only, this objective knowledge goes under the different names, *Mâyâ, avidyâ,* bondage, impurity, darkness, ignorance, the mind, the cycles of repeated births and deaths, etc.

D.: Be it so, what has this got to do with the extinction of the mind?

M.: Listen. You must understand that the knowledge signified by all these terms is only the mind.

32-33. *D.:* Who else says so?

M.: Vasishtha has said to Râma:

"Whatever objective knowledge manifests as this and that, or not this and not that, or in any other manner, it is only the mind. The mind is nothing but this manifest knowledge."

34. *D.:* Let it be so. How can the mind be extinguished?

M.: To forget everything is the ultimate means. But for thought, the world does not arise. Do not think and it will not arise. When nothing arises in the mind, the mind itself is lost. Therefore do not think of anything, forget all. This is the best way to kill the mind.

D.: Has any one else said so before?

M.: Vasishtha said so to Râma thus: "Efface thoughts of all kinds, of things enjoyed, not enjoyed, or otherwise. Like wood or stone, remain free from thoughts."

Râma: Should I altogether forget everything?

Vasishtha : Exactly ; altogether forget everything and remain like wood or stone.

Râma: The result will be dullness like that of stones or wood.

Vasishtha : Not so. All this is only illusion. Forgetting the illusion, you are freed from it. Though seeming dull, you will be the bliss Itself. Your intellect will be altogether clear and sharp. Without getting entangled in worldly life, but appearing active to others, remain as the very bliss of *Brahman* and be happy. Unlike the blue colour of the sky, let not the illusion of the world revive in the pure ether of Consciousness-Self. To forget this illusion is the sole means to kill the mind and remain as bliss. Though Shiva, Vishnu, or *Brahman* Himself should instruct you, realization is not possible without this one means. Without forgetting everything, fixity as the Self is impossible. Therefore altogether forget everything.

38-39. *D.:* Is it not very difficult to do so?

M.: Though for the ignorant it is difficult, for the discerning few it is very easy. Never think of anything but the unbroken unique *Brahman*. By a long practice of this, you will easily forget the non-self. It cannot be difficult to remain still without thinking anything. Let not thoughts arise in the mind; always think of *Brahman*. In this way all worldly thoughts will vanish and thought of *Brahman* alone will remain. When this becomes steady, forget even this, and without thinking, "I am *Brahman*", be the very *Brahman*. This cannot be difficult to practice.

40. Now my wise son, follow this advice; cease thinking of anything but *Brahman*. By this practice your mind will be extinct; you will forget all and remain as pure *Brahman*.

41. He who studies this chapter and follows the instructions contained therein, will soon be *Brahman* Itself!

APPENDIX I

Stages of	Viveka	Vairâgya	Uparati	Mumukshutva
Cause	Arises only in a purified mind.	Arises from *viveka*.	Results from *ashtânga yoga*.	Begins with *satsanga*, *i.e.*, association with realized sages.
Nature	To be convinced that *Brahman* alone is real and all else false.	Is to renounce the world and have no desire for anything in it.	Consists in restraining the mind.	Is to yearn for *mukti*.
Effect	Always to remember this truth.	Is to turn away in disgust from all enjoyments.	Is to cease from worldly activities.	Its effect is to remain with one's Master.
Limit	To be settled unswervingly in the truth that only *Brahman* is real.	Is treating with contempt all pleasures—earthly or heavenly.	Ends in forgetting the world because activities have ceased.	Ends in giving up of all *shâstras* and performance of religious rites.
Fruit	The unreality of the *jagat* results in *vairâgya*.	Peace.		

APPENDIX II

Stages	Jñâna (supreme Knowledge)	Shravana	Manana
Cause	Arises from shravana, manana nididhyâsana and samâdhi.	Results from viveka, vairâgya, uparati, mumukshutva.	Arises from viveka, i.e., in-direct knowledge.
Nature	It is the blissful state of shanti in which Brahman alone exists and nothing else.	Always to be hearing of the non-dual Brahman.	Enquiry into the truth of the advaitâtma.
Effect	Non-revival of the ego.	Removal of asattâvarana.	Removal of abhânâvarana.
Limit	As firmly convinced by realizing aham Brahmâsmi (I am Brahman).	Non-recurrence of astattâvarana.	Non-recurrence of abhânâvarana.
Fruit	Jivanmukti	Paroksha jñâna (indirect knowledge), i.e., capacity for distinguishing the real from the unreal.	Aparoksha jñâna (direct knowledge) i.e., clearly to distinguish the Self from the ego.

INDEX

Index

Cream of Liberation

Translation of *Kaivalya Navaneeta,*
an ancient Tamil classic
by Tandavaraya Swami

Translation into English by
Swami Sri Ramanananda Saraswathi

Preface to the 1965 Edition

We have great pleasure in offering to the devotees of Shri Bhagavân and the students of *Vedânta* in general, a valuable little classic. This was one of the works very frequently referred to by the Mahârshi.

In the absence of any mention in earlier literature on *Vedânta* in Tamil we can assume that *Kaivalya Navaneeta* was probably written at least five hundred years ago. It was translated into German and English by Dr. Charles Graul DD of the Leipzig Lutheran Mission, and we have in the Ramanasramam Library a book containing these German and English translations, published in 1855, both in Leipzig and London. We have not come across any other English translation so far.

We are confident that this great little book will prove to be of immense help to all *sâdhakas*.

T. N. Venkataraman
President Board of Trustees
Sri Ramanasramam

Introduction

The *Kaivalya Navaneeta* is a widely known *Advaita* classic in Tamil. *Navaneeta* means "butter." *Kaivalya* or *revala* is the state in which the soul exists, isolated from all connection with the body etc. From the vast ocean of milk (the *Upanishads,* etc.) the great teachers have drawn the milk of wisdom and filled it in pots (ancient texts). Tandavaraya Swâmi, the author of the *Kaivalya Navaneeta,* says that he has extracted the butter from the milk. Those who have obtained this (being fed on the butter of divine wisdom—*Brahma jñâna*—and being eternally satisfied) will not roam about feeding on dust (non-real objects of sense).

Verses 175 and 179 contain references to Nârâyana Desikar of Nannilam, as the preceptor of the author of this work. The author extols the greatness of his parents who had the prophetic insight to give him an appropriate name. *Tandava* is interpreted in the present context as one who was beckoned to leap across the sea of births as well as one who dances eternally in the delight resulting from divine wisdom.

The two sections of this work are called "The Exposition of the Truth" *(Tattva vilakkappadalam)* and "Doubts Cleared Away" *(Sandeham telitarppadalam).* They explain the basic philosophical principles and clear doubts which are likely to arise in understanding these principles.

In language easy to understand, the author gives a remarkably clear exposition of the tenets of *Advaita.* Its English translation will serve to make it known to a larger circle of readers and thus extend its usefulness.

V. A. DEVASENÂPATHI
Professor of Philosophy
University of Madras, 19th July, 1965

The Cream of Liberation

Kaivalya Navaneeta

1. Prostrations to the holy feet of the unique Lord who like ether remains as the sole witness in the hearts of all beings, whether they are swayed by desire for wealth, lands, and women, or are free from such desire; and who shines as the towering peak over the seven successive spiritual heights,[1] which are in themselves exalted over all other planes (of mind), or in Nannilam, the holiest of the seven holy places!

2. I worship the ever-shining pure Consciousness, which manifests as Brahmâ, Vishnu, or mighty Shiva, according as He creates, preserves or withdraws (the universe), and also as the countless individual beings, yet remains ever-free and perfect as the blazing sun over the ocean of Bliss.

3. I ever worship the lotus feet of my Master by whose grace I learnt that my very self is the all embracing Reality (*Brahman*) and the mosaic of the Universe but a phenomenon in me, and who remained as the Self, like the ether in a wall.

4. I adore the Almighty who manifested as my Master in order that the mind, the intellect, the senses and the body, might to my very knowledge be reduced to nothing, like mist before the sun, when He taught me "You and I are one," to make me one with Him!

5. I adore the feet of the holy Master who shines forth for ever as the wide expanse which has no beginning or end or interval, and I proceed to tell you the true nature of the Absolute Being, to explain bondage and liberation so that even those who are too dull to learn the scriptures, may understand.

---

1. See Section II, v. 149, and Appendix I.

6. All the ancient sages drew from the boundless Ocean of milk, namely the *Vedânta*[2] and filled their pitchers, their works.[3] I boiled them all (on the fire of the Master's words), churned them (with the churn of enquiry into the Self) and I present this Cream of Liberation—*Kaivalya Navaneeta*—to all.

Now, will those who have partaken of this and satisfied their hunger, roam about eating the offal of externals[4]?

7. After adoring my Master Venkatesa Mukunda, who is himself ever-free, and who made me his own, I write this *Kaivalya Navaneeta* divided into two parts, the first of which contains a clear exposition of the Truth,[5] and the second of which clears away all doubts arising from the former.[6]

2. The *Upanishads.*
3. The *sûtras,* the *itihâsas,* the *kâvyas* and *bhashyas.*
4. i.e., seek fulfillment of their desire for worldly life?
5. *Tattva-vilakkam.*
6. *Sandehantelithal.*

Section I

The Exposition of the Truth

8. The sages say that there are four prerequisites[7] for realization of the Truth: (1) *viveka*: discrimination between the temporary (therefore unreal phenomena) and the permanent (therefore the Reality, i.e., the noumenal); (2) indifference to the enjoyment of pleasures here or hereafter; (3) the group of six qualities; and (4) the longing for liberation.

9 & 10. The six qualities are *sama, dâmâ, uparati, titikshâ, samâdhâna* and *shraddhâ*. Of these, *sama* is control of mind; *dâmâ* is control of the senses; *uparati* is cessation of activities (relating to caste, creed, family, etc.); *titikshâ* is control of passions, and includes endurance; *samâdhâna* is, according to the sages, the settling down of the mind to reflect on the Truth, as revealed (by the scriptures and the sages); *shraddhâ* denotes faith in the Master and the scriptures. Such are the meanings of the six terms of this category.

11. No one can achieve anything in the world without being properly equipped for the task. For the same reason, only those who are equipped with these four categories of prerequisites can gain illumination. A novice cannot get it so readily. If so gained, it follows that the person has been successively purified in countless incarnations in the past.

12. He alone is fit for Knowledge, who, suffering from the three kinds of troubles rising from the self, the elements, and Providence (from hunger, thirst and so forth; from heat, cold, rain, disease, and the like; from robbers, wild animals, etc.) squirmed like a worm scorched by heat and panted for a dip in the nectar of wisdom so as to put an end to the series of rebirths.

---

7. *sâdhanâs.*

13. As the desire for liberation grew, he became unconcerned about his wife, children and property, ran away from them like an antelope which had extricated itself from the noose of a hunter, and sought a holy Master and respected him with all his heart.

14. After eagerly saluting his Master, he stood up and sobbed out his heart, saying, "O Lord! I have suffered long the torture of worldly life, which is after all so false! Gracious Master, save me by tearing off the cords which bind me to the five sheaths, so that my heart may be at peace!"

15. The Master lovingly considered him, like a tortoise its eggs; looked at him, like a fish its eggs; and passed his hands over him, like a bird its wings over its eggs, and said, "There is a means to put an end to your rebirths. I will tell you, and if you act upon it your rebirths will cease."[8]

16. At the very sound of the words, "your rebirths will cease," his frame thrilling, his heart rejoicing as if refreshed after a bath in a spacious tank, tears of joy flowing, like love welling forth, he held the holy feet of the Master and prayed further:

17. "Even if I, your servant, am unable to carry out your instructions, you can set me right by your grace. You said just now, 'There is a means to put an end to your re-births'! Kindly tell it to me and save me, I pray."

18. Finding[9] him self-subdued, the Master looks at the soul of the disciple, and begins to instruct him, so that it may regain its true nature, as a wasp places a well-chosen caterpillar in its cell of earth, and then buzzes before it.

19 & 20. "Look here, my son! He who has forgotten his true nature is alternately born and dies, turning round and round in

8. This symbolizes the three kinds of initiation: by thought, by look and by touch.
9. The change of tense is in the original text.

the unceasing wheel of time, like a feather caught up in a whirl-wind, until he realizes the true nature of the Self. If he comes to see the individual self and its substratum, the Overself, then he becomes the substratum, i.e., *Brahman*, and escapes rebirths. Should you know yourself, no harm will befall you. As you asked I have told you this."

21. *Disciple:* Lord, do you take me for a fool that you tell me so? Can there be any in the world who are ignorant of the self? How then are they all caught up in the cycle of births and deaths? Tell me the unerring Truth for I beseech you in full faith.

22. *Master:* Only he is Self-realized who knows what is the body and who is embodied.

Disciple: Who else is embodied but this gross thing?

On this, the Master smiled in pity, and spoke:

23. "You say that you cannot find the embodied being as different from the gross body. Then tell me who appeared as the subject in your dream; or who experienced the sleep in which even the pain of dream was absent; or again what is this consciousness in the waking state?"

24. *Disciple:* Every day experience proves that the experiencer in the waking state, or the experiencer of dreams when the waking consciousness is gone, or the experiencer of deep slumber, must be different (from the gross body). Yet it is not realized. It just flashes in the mind, only to fade away at once. Please explain this.

25. Just as people pointing to a tree on the earth mark the third day crescent moon, and pointing to other stars locate Arundhati, so also the sage began pointing to the gross in order to make known the subtle cause.

26. *Master:* The *Vedânta* as a whole mentions as the cause of bondage and release, superimposition[10] and its effacement,[11] respectively. Bondage is caused by superimposition; release by its effacement.

Now listen as regards the former.

27. Superimposition is seeing one thing in another: a snake, for instance, in a rope, a man in a post, water in a mirage, or a blue canopy in the empty sky.

28. Similarly, the five elements and their combinations seen in *Brahman*—which is free from name and form, one and the same without a second, self-conscious and perfect—are products of illusion.

29. If you ask how superimposition gives rise to creation (the answer is):

The beginningless[12] *jîvas* remain unmanifest in *avyakta,* as in deep slumber. This state (is disturbed) by the generative thought of *Îshvara,* otherwise called Time. Then *avyakta* ceases to be causal (i.e., latent) and the three *gunâs* manifest.

30. They are *sattva, rajas* and *tamas,* which are pure white, red, and black, respectively; or again, clear, turbid, and dark. Though equal, one of them will always predominate.

31. This is one explanation. Another is as follows: The causal state, which remains unmanifest, later expands as *mahâtattva* (the totality of the *jîvas*) and manifests as the ego wherein the three *gunâs* become apparent.

32. Ether-like *Chit* is reflected in them. Of the three, *sattva* is

---

10. *Âropa*—erroneous knowledge, false attribution, or illusion.
11. *Apavâda.*
12. Whose beginning cannot be known.

clear, and is called *Mâyâ*. *Brahman* reflected in this is *Îshvara*, the intelligent cause of the universe, immanent in all, untainted by *Mâyâ* or by any of the *gunâs*.

33. This *Mâyâ* is the state of deep slumber, the causal body, and the blissful sheath of *Îshvara*. *Rajoguna* is *avidyâ* (absence of real knowledge). *Chit* reflected in this *guna* (which is not clear owing to its constant agitation), gives rise to countless beings. The *jîva* in this state is known as *prâjña*.

34. This is the blissful sheath, the state of deep sleep, and the causal body of the *jîvas*. I have so far described the causal stage of superimposition.

Hear me now explain its subtle phase.

35. To provide the wherewithal of experience to the *jîvas*, by the loving grace of *Îshvara* who has all the wondrous powers of His inseparable *Mâyâ*, the *tamoguna* then divides itself into its two aspects, namely: (1) dense veiling of Reality[13]; and (2) multiplicity of phenomena.[14]

36. In the latter of these two, there appears ether; from ether, air; from air, fire; from fire, water; from water, earth. All these five, in the nascent state, are called elements. From these arise bodies suitable for experiences.

37. The three *gunas* permeate all these five elements. In *sattva*, which is pure, there arise the *jñânendriyas*,[15] of individual function, and also the mind and intellect, of collective function. These seven products of *sattva* form the instruments of knowledge.

38. Then in *rajoguna* there arise the vital airs,[16] of collective

13. *Âvarana.*
14. *Vikshepa.*
15. The senses of hearing, sight, touch, taste and smell.
16. *Prâna, apâna, vyâna, udâna* and *samâna.*

function, and the *karmendriyas*,[17] of individual function. These seventeen[18] fundamentals form the subtle bodies of gods, demons, human beings, animals, and all other living organisms.

39. The *jîva*, united to such a body, is called *taijasa*; and *Îshvara*, under similar conditions, is known as *Hiranyagarbha*. In both cases it is called the *lingasharîra* or the subtle body which comprises the three sheaths (the vital, the mental and the intellectual). This is their dream-state.

40. So much for the subtle body. Now hear me describe the process of superimposition of the gross body.
Îshvara, who is ever watchful, combined the five elements so as to evolve gross bodies for the *jîvas*, and objects for experience.
41. Each of the five elements was divided into two halves; each half was subdivided into four quarters. Then the major half of one element was combined with one quarter subdivision of each of the other four. This process gave rise to the gross elements from which the four classes of beings,[19] and their experiences, the universe and its worlds, were created.

42. The *jîva*, united with the gross body, is called *vishva*; and *Îshvara* under similar conditions, is known as *virât*. The gross body is the physical sheath,[20] and their waking state. Remember this brief statement regarding the gross body.

43. *Disciple:* Master! If these states[21] be common to both, how shall we know the difference between exalted *Îshvara* and the ordinary *jîva?*
Master: The *jiva* is the effect and *Îshvara* the cause. There is also a difference as between units and their totality.

17. Hands, feet, organs of speech, of excretion and of reproduction.
18. The ten principles mentioned here and the seven contained in the previous stanza.
19. (1) Foetus-born, (2) egg-born, (3) larva-born, and (4) seed-born.
20. *Annamaya-kosha*, among the *pancha-koshas*.
21. The gross, subtle and causal states, which form the *upâdhis*.

44. The trees form the units; their aggregate is the forest. Generally speaking the mobile and immobile *jîvas* are the separate units; their sum total is *Îshvara*. This is the difference between *Îshvara* and the *jîvas*.

45. I have said thus far what superimposition is. Only he is a *jñâni* who knows beyond doubt that all that is seen is only ephemeral like a dream.

Now, listen to the process of effacement of superimposition, the way to wonderful *moksha*[22] which resembles the placid sky when all the clouds of winter clear away.

46. (Just as one examines and finds out that) this is not a snake but a rope, and this is not a thief but a thick post, so also one makes out beyond doubt, by the word of the Master and the light of the scriptures, that the body, the world and the elements are only *Brahman*, i.e., unchanging Consciousness. Know this to be the effacement of superimposition.

47. Cause and effect are the same, like cloth and yarn, ornaments and gold, utensils and clay. To resolve the body into its antecedent cause, until *avidyâ* is traced as the root-cause of all, is the method of effacing superimposition.

48. *Disciple:* You have said that the *tamoguna* functions in two aspects, namely veiling and multiplicity, of which you have explained the latter, which springs from desire. Tell me, my Lord, the result of the other aspect—veiling.

49. *Master: Âvarana*[23] veils the inner vision of all embodied beings, except unexcelled *Îshvara* and self-realised *jñânis*, in the shape of: "It is not; It does not shine forth," in the same way as the dense darkness of a wintry night hides the sky, the earth and the directions from our view.

22. Liberation.
23. i.e., the veiling power.

50. Outwardly this altogether obstructs the distinguishing of *Brahman* who is Perfection, from His modifications (as the world), and inwardly that of the Self which is pure Consciousness, from Its modifications (as the inner faculties, i.e., the ego, the mind). It is therefore the sole cause of that chronic disease, the endless series of births and deaths.

51. The question then arises: Whereon does the superimposition rest when the substratum is completely hidden? And how can there be any superimposition if the substratum is not hidden? (The answer is:) The substratum is twofold: general and particular, of which the general substratum remains continuous and unbroken. Transient superimposition is particular.

52. In the world, the common substratum, "This is," can never be veiled; but only the particular identity, "This is a rope." Similarly with the *jîva*: ignorance[24] does not veil the substratum, "I am"; but it does veil the specific knowledge, "I am Brahman."

53. *Disciple:* How does it happen, my Master, that the power of veiling is censured for the doings of the power of multiplicity, which arising as the five sheaths, the *jîva* and the world, obstructs pure Being from view?

Master: Listen to me in answer to this question.

54. Although the power of multiplicity is the direct cause of the misery-laden cycle of births (and deaths), yet it is of service to those who seek liberation in earnest. Can the darkness of night be of the same service for one's useful activities as the light of day? What more can I say to you? Therefore, my son, the power of veiling is the more harmful of the two.

---

24. The knowledge, "This is" persists whether we see a rope or a snake: it is unbroken, continuous and general; whereas there is no knowledge of a rope when it is seen as a snake, nor of a snake when it is seen as a rope. Such knowledge is real when a rope is recognized, and unreal when a snake is presumed.

55. Has any one gained release from the cycle of subsequent births because the world was totally lost from view in his deep sleep or in the dissolution? The power of multiplicity can altogether bring about liberation, but the thick veil of ignorance is the sole cause of the present calamity.

56. You may argue thus: Since the power of multiplicity is said to be a superimposition like the appearance of silver in mother-of-pearl and is therefore false, the liberation gained by the aid of this false power must also be equally false. (The answer is:) A frightful dream, though unreal, ends in waking up the dreamer from sleep. Even so, liberation is real.

57. Just as poison is commonly antidoted with another poison, an iron spike is extracted with another (piece of) iron, arrows are turned aside by others, and dirt is washed away with other dirt (e.g., fuller's earth), so ignorance which is weak in itself, can be eradicated by methods which are themselves of the same *Mâyâ*; later this also perishes like the pole used to turn a corpse that is burnt.

58. Through this *Mâyâ*, *jîva*s experience seven stages of development as follows: ignorance,[25] veiling,[26] multiplicity,[27] indirect knowledge,[28] direct experience,[29] freedom from misery,[30] and supreme Bliss.[31]

59 & 60. Of these, ignorance is to lose sight of the fact that the inner self is no other than *Brahman*; veiling makes one say: "There is no *Brahman*. I do not see Him"; multiplicity springs up as, "I am a man. I am a *jîva*"; indirect knowledge is to know the nature of the Self by the teachings of the Master; direct experience is to stay unshaken as the unitary Being after

25. *Avidyâ.*
26. *Âvarana.*
27. *Vikshepa.*
28. *Paroksha jñâna.*
29. *Aparoksha jñâna.*
30. *Duhkha nivritti.*
31. *Sukha avâpti.*

enquiry into the Self; freedom from misery is to end limitations and the sense of doership; and supreme Bliss is the final accomplishment, i.e., release from bondage.

61. I shall now relate to you a story to illustrate this: Ten men forded a stream and, on reaching the other shore, each of them counted nine others and omitted to count himself. They were all perplexed (because the tenth man was missing).

62 & 63. Ignorance is want of right understanding, which causes confusion. "The tenth man is missing, not to be found." This thought is the veiling. Grief at the loss of the companion *vikshepa*. To heed the words of a sympathetic passer-by who says: "The tenth man is among you," is indirect knowledge. When the kindly man further makes one of them count the others and points to the teller as the tenth man, the discovery of oneself as the missing tenth man forms direct experience. The cessation of grief for the lost man is freedom from misery. The joy of indubitable ascertainment by oneself is supreme Bliss.

64. The disciple prayed: "Lord, Master! Pray show me my real Self so that I may know It as truly as the tenth man did in the anecdote."

Master: There is the *mahâvâkya*, "That thou art." The verb "art" in it establishes the identity of the pronouns "That" and "thou" in their ultimate meaning. I shall explain how it does so. Hear me.

65. Just as the ether, though single, is fourfold, as the wide expanse, the ether in the clouds, the ether in the pot, and the reflection in water, so *chit,* which is single, is called the all-pervading *Brahman, Îshvara,* the self, and the *jîva.*

66. In the *mahâvâkya* referred to, the word "That" stands for almighty *Îshvara* and "thou" stands for the *jîva.* But ultimately they mean respectively *Brahman,* who is free from *Mâyâ,* and the

inner Self who is free from limitations. They are now mutually bound up like butter in boiled milk. Just as the milk is churned and the butter separated, so also you should realize the Self and thus stand apart.

67. The way to get rid of the trappings (of the *jîva*) is to kill the present idea that "I am the body," which is only a corpse after all, for it is a mere assemblage of the five elements. Nor can you be the breath which moves through the nostrils like the blasts of air blown by bellows. It is simply a function of *rajoguna*.

68. Can the Self be the intellect or the mind which stand to each other in the relation of agent and instrument? These two sheaths are only modes of *sattvaguna*. Let not the unedifying bliss of deep sleep be mistaken for the Self, for it is only a mode of *tamoguna*.

69. Know "thou," as the Self, to be *Sat, Chit, Ânanda,* the ever unchanging, single, eternal and all-pervading Witness, and rid yourself of the trap of the five sheaths which are of an opposite nature—false, insentient, painful, etc.

70. *Disciple:* When I dissociate myself from the five sheaths and look beyond, there remains only a blank. I see nothing more than that. Am I to take this blank for the supreme experience of the Self? Tell me this truly, my Master.

71. On this request of the disciple, the Master further said: "In the anecdote the tenth man, of deluded intellect, after counting only nine men and not recognizing himself as the tenth, was stupefied. Can such stupor be the tenth man? Good son! You are the seer of all (i.e., the blank and the five sheaths).

72. By the Lord under the sacred banyan tree! I speak the truth: You are the unchanging Witness of the gross, subtle and (causal) ignorance, the waking, dream and sleep states, and the passage of time—past, present and future, which endlessly rise and fall, like waves in the ocean of bliss.

73. Do not ask: 'By what light shall I see myself who am the all-seeing witness?' Can there be a light to illumine the self-luminous Light? The tenth man knows himself as such among the others. Is there an eleventh man in him?

74. To argue that knowledge is necessary to make knowledge known, is foolish and leads to interminable controversy. You are neither known nor unknown. Realize yourself as Self-shining Knowledge.

75. Is it what makes the sweets sweet not the nature of sugar to be sweet? Realize yourself as the meaning of 'I', which makes known objects as 'this' and 'that'[32] and Itself lies beyond them.

76. The Self, as described above, is the primary meaning of 'thou' (in the *mahâvâkya:* 'That thou art'). *Brahman,* which is never bound by limitations, is the primary meaning of 'That'. Their secondary meanings are the transient *jîva* and *Îshvara,* respectively. Two separate entities can never be identical.

77. The distinctions between *Îshvara* and the *jîva* are due to their names, localities, artificial limitations, bodies and capacities. They are as far apart as the upper and the nether regions. Their identity is unthinkable with these associations.

78. When the conventional acceptations of terms appear inconsistent, the pandits of ancient lore bring out the true meanings by employing three methods of exegesis: disjunction, conjunction or the two combined.[33]

79. (1) 'The house on the Ganges';[34] and (2) 'The black remained and the red fled';[35] and (3) 'This is that Devadatta,' are (respective) examples of the above. The apparent contradictions in several scriptural passages are eliminated by a judi-

32. Or: "the seen" and "the unseen."
33. *Jahat lakshana, ajahat lakshana* and *jahadajahat lakshana.*
34. Meaning the house on the shore of the Ganges, not on the waters of the river.
35. Meaning the black cows remained and the red horses fled.

cious use of these three exegetical methods.*

80. In the example: 'This is that Devadatta,' the man who was seen in another place and on another occasion, and also known as Devadatta, is this man who is seen in this place and on this occasion. Although the time and place are different, a little consideration reveals the man to be the same.

81. Similarly, in the words 'That' and 'thou,' their literal meanings excluded, the Consciousness-Principle is taken as *Brahman* and as the Witness, whose unbroken identity is established by 'art,' so that *Brahman* is the Self, and the Self is *Brahman.*

82. The ether reflected in water in a pot, and in the clouds[36] are both circumstantial and therefore unreal, whereas the space in the pot and the wide expanse are together one and the same. Similarly, all-pervading *Brahman* and the Witness in the individual being are together one and the same. You must experience it so that you may remain fixed in the realization, 'I am the Reality.'

83. On hearing this, the disciple, loyal to the instructions of the Master discarded the five sheaths and the blank, realized the Self as "I am Brahman," went beyond that and remained as perfect Being.

84. At the glance of the Master who was grace incarnate, the worthy disciple sank into the ocean of Bliss and merged as the undivided Whole, as pure Consciousness free from the body, organs and all else, with mind made perfect so that he became the true Self, unaware while awake.

* Translator Note: Here only the last is applicable.
36. The ether is invisible. But the region in which the clouds are, is marked off in our vision. It is therefore said to be the ether reflected in the clouds.

85. After the blessed disciple had remained in that state for a long time, his mind gently turned outward. Then he saw his glorious Master before him. His eyes were filled with tears of joy. He was full of love and fell at the feet of the Master. He rose up, came round the Master and with folded hands spoke to him:

86. "Lord, you are the Reality remaining as my inmost Self, ruling me during all my countless incarnations! Glory to you who have put on an external form in order to instruct me! I do not see how I can repay your Grace for having liberated me. Glory! Glory to your holy feet!"

87. The Master beamed on him as he spoke, drew him near and said very lovingly: "To stay fixed in the Self, without the three kinds of obstacles obstructing your experience, is the highest return you can render me."

88. Disciple: My Lord! Can such realization as has transcended the dual perception of 'you' and 'I', and found the Self to be entire and all-prevading, fail me at any time?

Master: The truth, 'I am *Brahman*', is realized from the scriptures or by the grace of the Master, but it cannot be firm in the face of obstructions.

89. Ignorance, uncertainty and wrong knowledge, are obstacles resulting from long-standing habits in the innumerable incarnations of the past which cause trouble, and then the fruits of realization slip away. Therefore root them out by hearing the Truth, reasoning and meditation.[37]

90. Checked by incantations,[38] fire will not scorch. Likewise defective realization will not put an end to bondage. Therefore devote yourself to hearing the Truth, reasoning and meditation and root out ignorance, uncertainty and wrong knowledge.

37. *Shravana, manana* and *nididhyâsana.*
38. *Sthambhana.*

91. Ignorance veils the Truth that the Self is *Brahman* and shows forth multiplicity instead; uncertainty is the confusion resulting from lack of firm faith in the words of the Master; the illusion that the evanescent world is a reality and that the body is the self is wrong knowledge. So say the sages.

92. Hearing the Truth is to revert the mind repeatedly to the teaching: 'That thou art.' Reasoning is rational investigation of the meaning of the text, as already heard. Meditation is one-pointedness of mind. If every day you do these, you will surely gain liberation.

93. The practice must be kept up so long as the sense of knower and knowledge persists. No effort is necessary thereafter. Remaining as pure, eternal Consciousness, untainted like the ether and thus liberated while alive, one will live forever as 'That,' after being disembodied also.

94. The wise, remaining like ether and liberated even here, are of four classes, namely *Brahmavid* (i.e., a knower of *Brahman*), *vara, varya,* and *varishta,* in order of merit.

95. The *Brahmavid*s, who by steadfast practice have gained clear realization of *Brahman,* continue to perform even the hard duties[39] of their caste and stage in life, exactly as prescribed by the *shâstras,* for the benefit of others, without themselves swerving from their supreme state.

96. Should passions rise up they disappear instantly and cannot taint the mind of the *Brahmavid*s who live in society detached like water on a lotus leaf. They look ignorant, not showing forth their knowledge, and remain mute owing to the intensity of inward Bliss.

97. *Prârabdha,* i.e., *karma* which is now bearing fruit, differs according to the actions in past incarnations. Therefore the

---

39. *Varnâshrama dharma.*

present pursuits also differ among *jñânis*, who are all, however, liberated even here. They may perform holy *tapas*; or engage in trade and commerce; or rule a kingdom; or wander about as mendicants.

98. They would not think of the past or future; would partake of what comes unsolicited; would not wonder, even if the sun turned into the moon, or at any other marvel, whether the sky were to spread its shoots down like a banyan tree or a corpse were to be revived; nor would they distinguish good and bad, for they always remain as the unchanging Witness of all.

99. Among the other three classes, the *vara* and the *varya* remain settled in *samâdhi*. The *vara* feels concern for the maintenance of the body; the *varya* is reminded of it by others; the *varishta* never becomes aware of the body either by himself or through others.

100. Although there are distinguishing characteristics in the lives of the different sages, who are themselves very rare in the world, yet there is absolutely no difference in the experience of liberation. What can be the use of the hard-won *samâdhi*? The *Brahmavid*, who is outwardly active, seems sometimes to feel the misery of calamities, whereas the others remain in unbroken Bliss.

101. Now, if the *Brahmavid*s live like the ignorant, how are they free from the cycle of births, and how is their ignorance gone?
  The all-pervading ether remains untainted by anything; the other four elements are tainted by contact with objects. So it is with the *Brahmavid* and the ignorant.

102. The immemorial *Vedas* declare that single-minded devotion to a holy sage is not only pleasing to Brahmâ, Vishnu and Shiva together, but also secures the rewards of all the *Vedic* rites, and finally liberation from the cycle of births.

Now listen how liberation while alive persists after disembodiment also.

103. Manifold *karma* in store, gathered in many births, is altogether burnt away in the fire of *jñâna*, like cotton in a huge conflagration. Further accumulating *karma* can never approach the *jñâni*. The *karma* which has brought about the present incarnation is exhausted by experiencing its fruits.

104. How will the merits and demerits of actions during his experience of *prârabdha* cease to affect him later on? His detractors share the demerits, and his devotees the merits.

105. The causal body of ignorance is reduced to ashes in the fire of rare *jñâna*; the visible gross body becomes a corpse in due course; then like a drop of water on red-hot iron, the subtle body is dissolved in the Self which underlies these three bodies and remains entire all along.

106. As soon as the entity of a pot is broken up, the ether in the pot becomes indistinguishable from the all-pervading ether. So also when the limitation of the body is gone, the *jîvanmukta* reverts to the natural eternal disembodied state of liberation, free from beginning, middle or end and in or out.

107. Just as the ether, though all-pervading, seems to be newly opened in a well which is newly dug, so *Brahman*, though ever-present, yet appears as if realized afresh by enquiry into the Self as taught by a Master or the scriptures. Therefore, O son, be at peace. We are always the same limitless Being!

108. The whole universe is as unreal as water in a mirage, silver in mother-of-pearl, the city of *Gandharvas* in the air, the dreamland of dream, the blue of the sky, the serpent in a rope, the off-spring of a barren woman, the horn of a hare, or the thief in a thick post. O son! Pure Consciousness is alone real. Do not therefore forget the Self at any moment."

Thus ends the First Section of *Kaivalya Navaneeta*.

Section II

Doubts Cleared Away

1. *Master.* Just as men dig a hole, gently plant a long post in it, fill in earth, and ram it in, to fix it firmly, so too, I take to clearing away doubts, that your mind, which has realized the Self as being the supreme Consciousness, may remain unshaken.

2. The disciple, pure minded and Self-realized, clung to his Master from the time of wrong identification of the self with the body, to the moment of unmoded, unembodied liberation, like a young monkey to its mother.

3. Finding that the loving disciple keeps to him like his shadow, the Master asks him: "Are you able to stay unshaken as a mere witness? Have all your doubts disappeared? Or, does the sense of differentiation creep in at times? Tell me your condition."

4. On this the disciple bowed to the feet of the Master and said: "Father, dare the phantoms of differentiation, which can roam about only in the darkness of ignorance, in the wilderness of worldly life, appear to the inner vision in the broad daylight of wisdom after the sun of your teaching has risen over the summit of your grace?

5. Even after the devil is exorcised, just as the person who was possessed is further protected by a talisman against any return of the trouble, so also, though my ignorance has already been dispelled by your teaching, yet, sir, I seek more from you that I may be firmly fixed in the Self.

6. You were pleased to say, 'Know it from the scriptures (that

the Self is *Brahman*), non-dual *Brahman* cannot be reached by speech (study or discussion). It must be realized in the heart. Self-shining *Brahman* cannot be reached by the miserable mind.' Please clear what seems to be the contradiction of these two statements.

7. *Master:* As *Brahman* is neither an object of the senses, nor an object of inference, and as there is no second to It, It is beyond direct perception, inference or analogy.[1] Also know that being free from attributes, It cannot be expressed by words.

8. The *Vedas*, which declare that *Brahman* lies beyond words, also signify It by the text ("That thou art"). If you ask which is right, know that both are right for the *Vedas* can never be untrue.

9. A girl says, "not he," "not he" of all others, and remains shy and silent when her lover is pointed out. In the same way, the *Vedas* clearly deny what is not *Brahman*, as "not this," "not this," and indicate *Brahman* by silence.

10. Having answered the first part of your question, I proceed to answer the second.
The heart governs the external senses. Its faculties operate, internally and externally, as intellect and mind.

11. As your face is seen reflected in a mirror, so the image of pure Consciousness[2] is seen in intellect. Along with this, mind proceeds to function, and this is called knowledge, my good son!

12. As molten metal takes the shapes of the mould into which it is poured, so the mind assumes the shapes of the objects, and they are revealed by the reflected light. Without eyesight and

1. *Pratyaksha, anumâna* and *upamâna.*
2. *Chit-âbhâsa.*

light, an object in darkness cannot be discovered.[3]

13. The aid of a burning lamp and clear eyesight are required to discover an object in darkness. But to see the sun, eyesight alone will do. To see the manifest universe, both moded mind[4] and reflected consciousness are necessary. But to realize the Reality, moded mind eager for realization will alone serve.

14. The union of the moded mind and the reflected self is called the mind. *Brahman* can be reached by the mind for the reason that the mode of mind directed to itself is necessary for realization. *Brahman* cannot be reached by that part of the mind which is reflected consciousness. Thus, reconciling the meaning, be free from doubt.

15. *Disciple:* Worthy Master of unerring wisdom, I have understood your teaching so far. Please let me ask you another question: Free from movement, unbroken, perfect, and transformed into "That", is not such a state of mind called *samâdhi yoga* (or Union in Peace)? How can this mind, always moving like a wing, and raising up several worlds in a trice, be stilled so that it may remain steady in the Self, like a flame protected from drafts? Tell me kindly.

16. *Master:* The active mind is composed of three *gunas*. When one of them is uppermost, the other two lie covert. With *sattvaguna,* divine qualities manifest; with *rajoguna,* tendencies pertaining to the world, the body and the *shâstras* manifest;[5] with *tamoguna,* the evil nature[6] manifests.

17. *Sattva* is the very nature of the mind, whereas the other two qualities are mere adjuncts and can therefore be banished

---

3. Light removes darkness, but the object must be seen by the eye. Similarly the modes of mind are objects which are illumined by the reflected light of the mind.
4. *Vritti.*
5. *Loka vâsanâ, deha vâsanâ* and *shâstra vâsanâ.*
6. *Âsurî sampat.*

from it. If one holds steadily to one's divineness, *rajas* and *tamas* will get strangled, so that the internal stresses and the external manifold disappear. When this happens, your mind shines forth untainted and becomes motionless and subtle like the ether. And then it naturally becomes one with *Brahman*, which is already so, and remains in undifferentiated peace *(nirvikalpa samâdhi)*.

18. When one stainless mirror is placed in front of another similar one, the reflecting surfaces will be one undistinguishable whole. Similarly, when the mind, which is clear, has become one with the infinite *sat-chit-ânanda Brahman*, and remains untainted, how can there be the manifold or movements in the mind? Tell me.

19. *Disciple:* How then can the wise, liberated while alive, exhaust their *prârabdha* if their mind has lost itself in *Brahman* and become one with It? Is it not done only by experiencing its results? Such experience would certainly require the mind. There cannot be any kind of experience in the absence of the mind. If the mind persists, how can it be said to be liberated? I am confused on this point. Be pleased to clear this doubt of mine, for I cannot be liberated unless all my doubts are cleared away.

20. *Master:* The annihilation of the mind is of two grades: namely, of the mind pattern[7] and of the mind itself.[8] The former applies to sages liberated while alive; the latter to disembodied sages. Elimination of *rajas* and *tamas*, leaving *sattva* alone, is the dissolution of the pattern of the mind, O sinless one! When *sattva* vanishes along with the subtle body, the mind itself is said to have perished too.

21. *Sattva* is pure and forms the very nature of the mind; when *rajas* and *tamas* (which give the pattern to it) are destroyed

7. *Sarûpa:* lit. *in its form.*
8. *Arûpa:* lit. (the mind) *which has no form.*

140

(by proper practice), the identity of the term "mind" is lost. For, in such a state, the sages will partake of what comes unsolicited to them; not think of the past or future; nor exult in joy or lament in sorrow; getting over their doership and becoming non-doers; witnessing the mental modes and the three states[9] they can remain liberated at the same time as they pass through *prârabdha*. There is no contradiction in it. You need have no doubts on this point.

22. On hearing that the whole period of activity is also the state of peace, you may object, saying, "Does not action denote changing mind, and on such change does not peace slip away?"

The state of the sage is like that of a girl who never ceases to thrill with love for her paramour even while she attends to her duties at home.

23. *Disciple:* Should the sage, liberated while alive, who has transcended the incidents of the body,[10] lost the sense of doership and the whole individuality, and become one with *Brahman*, be said to be the experiencer of *prârabdha*, he must also be the doer. Can there be experience to a perfect non-doer? Master who removes all misery! Please elucidate this point.

Master: Hear their greatness as perfect doers, perfect enjoyers and perfect renouncers:

24. As a hill of lodestone neither moves of itself nor puts things in motion, and yet pieces of iron orient themselves towards it, I neither act by myself nor actuate others, and yet the whole world is active before me. Like the sun, I remain an unconcerned witness of all the functions of the body, senses, etc., and also of the state of peace resulting from the merging of the mind in *Brahman*. One possessed of this firm experience is the perfect doer.

9. The waking, dream and dreamless sleep states.
10. The subtle and the gross bodies; caste, creed and so on.

25. The perfect enjoyer is he who partakes of anything that comes his way without discriminating whether it be tasty or not, clean or unclean, healthy or unhealthy, like a blazing fire consuming all that lies in its way. He whose mind is crystal clear, unaffected by passing phases, great or small, good or bad, his own or others, is the perfect renouncer. A liberated sage is strictly an exemplar of these three virtues (united).

26. *Disciple:* How can it be reckoned that the task of the sage is finished[11] if by *prârabdha* he lives on in a body acting and teaching to suit others desirous of liberation? O Master who so graciously removed the cause of my misery! Kindly answer me.

27. *Master:* Occupations of people are of three kinds: those pertaining to the present life and those pertaining to the here-after are only for the ignorant, possessed by desire for enjoyment,[12] sense of ownership[13] and attachment to the body. Only those who long for deliverance turn to the learning of the Truth, etc. Is there anything to be gained by learning or other similar actions for a person who is all-perfect?

28. *Disciple:* O crest jewel among Masters! Hear me. It is right that they alone can practice true wisdom who have deliberately discarded the joys of life here and hereafter. Can those who have turned away from worldly activities and rituals, to tread the path of liberation, ever turn back to the old methods?
Are not hearing, reasoning and meditation necessary to make the mind firm? Tell me truly!

29. *Master:* Wise son, hear me. They who do not know must learn the Truth (as taught by the scriptures and Masters); those who have doubts must engage in reasoning; those who are in the grip of wrong knowledge must practice meditation. Can

11. *Kritakritya.*
12. *Bhôgecchâ.*
13. *Mamata.*

there be anything wanting for those who have become the real, ethereal Being-Consciousness-Perfection?

30. *Disciple:* Lord, hear me! Can the wise also say like the ignorant, "I did; I saw; I ate," and "I went"? You say that they are free from wrong knowledge. Can realization of *Brahman*, which is real, admit of such expression? Please enlighten me on this point.

31. *Master.* A person who wakes up from a dream speaks of his experiences in the dream. In the same way, the Self-realized sage, though using the language of the ignorant, is not bound as the ego. A man who commits himself to the flames on the eve of his becoming an immortal god is spoken of only as a man, until his body is reduced to ashes. So also, the ego-free sage appears to function like others until he is disembodied.

32. *Disciple.* If so, O Master, though the objects are unreal, would not the transactions (associated with them) cause misery? Can they bestow the bliss of Knowledge? It can be felt only in their absence. Is it not necessary to be one-pointed? And if the person practices it, can he be said to have finished his task?

33. *Master.* Self-realized son! Activities end when *prârabdha* ends. Is not practice of *samâdhi* or worldly work an activity of the mind? Being one with the transcendent Self, can he do anything different from It? Should he be practicing *samâdhi*,[14] he cannot be said to be established in the Self.

34. *Disciple:* Master supreme! How is it then that some of those who are established in the Self, and have nothing more to do, practice mind-restraining meditations?

Master: I have already told you that the sages, liberated while

14. There are said to be six kinds of *samâdhi*.

alive, appear to be active in many ways according to their *prârabdha*.

35. My good boy, hear me further. The activities of the sage are solely for the uplift of the world. He does not stand to lose or gain anything. The Almighty, who is only the store of grace for the world, is not affected by the merit or demerit of the creation, etc.

36. *Disciple:* O Master, you who are formless (transcendentally), function as *Îshvara* (cosmically), and appear in human form (here)! You speak of a *jñâni* and *Îshvara* as the same. How can they be so?

Master: Yes. *Îshvara* and the *jñâni* are the same because they are free from "I" and "mine." The *jñâni* is himself *Îshvara*, the totality of the *jîva*s, and also the cosmos.

37. *Disciple:* Lord, if as you say he is all *jîva*s when he is liberated, how can others remain bound? If the *jîva*s are said to be diverse, he cannot be all. All-knowing Master! Please answer me this question in detail.

38 & 39. *Master:* The Self, which shines forth as "I-I" in all, is perfect and impartite. But *jîva*s are as diverse as the limitations formed by the ego. Look how the moon, who delights the world, is only one, whereas her reflected images are as many as there are ponds, pools, tanks, streams, cisterns and pitchers of water. Where one of them is destroyed, the image is no longer reflected, but is reabsorbed in its original, namely the moon. It cannot be so with the other reflected images. In the same manner, the *jîva* whose limitations are destroyed is withdrawn into its source, the Self, others not.

40. *Disciple:* How can a *jñâni* be the same as *Îshvara*, who is Brahmâ, Vishnu, and Shiva, the Lords of creation, preservation, and destruction of the universe? They can divine the thoughts

of others, know the past, present[15] and future, and are immanent in all. O Master of immense austerities! I do not find even a trace of these qualities in the *jñâni*.

41. *Master:* The water in a tank, and a powerful light, help the whole village, whereas a pot of water and a table-lamp help only the family circle in a home. O son in the company of the wise! *Îshvara* and the *jñâni* do not differ in their *jñâna*.[16] However, associated with the limitations of *Mâyâ*, they are spoken of as superior and inferior.

42. Like the kings and the *siddhas*[17] among men, the gods, such as Nârâyana, have some extraordinary powers like *anima*,[18] etc., because of their extraordinary antecedent austerities. Although men do not possess these powers and therefore appear less, yet from the standpoint of *Brahman* there is not the least difference between them.

43. *Disciple:* O Master who has caused my deliverance! Although there have been many sages in the world who possessed these extraordinary powers like *anima* (minuteness), etc., you say these powers are *Îshvara*'s own. Please make the matter clear to me.

15. Even remote or hidden.
16. Wisdom, namely the realization, "I am *Brahman*."
17. Adepts who have acquired the knowledge of everything past and future, remote or hidden; they divine the thoughts of others; gain the strength of an elephant, the courage of a lion, and the swiftness of the wind; fly in the air, float on water, dive into the earth, contemplate all worlds at a glance, and perform other strange feats.
18. The powers are eight:
    1. *Anima:* Shrinking to a minute form;
    2. *Mahimâ:* Enlargement to a gigantic size;
    3. *Laghimâ:* Levitating (e.g., rising along a sunbeam to the solar orb);
    4. *Prâkâmya:* Possessing unlimited reach of the organs (as touching the moon with the tip of a finger);
    5. *Garima:* Irresistible will (for instance, sinking into the earth as easily as in water);
    6. *Îsitâ:* Dominion over all beings animate or inanimate;
    7. *Vasitâ:* Faculty of changing the course of nature; and
    8. *Prâpti:* Ability to accomplish everything desired.

Master: Know that the powers are the fruits of their devotion to the glorious almighty Being, their austerities,[19] and practices of *yoga*.[20]

44. *Disciple:* O Shiva in the form of my Master! If these powers and deliverance are together the fruits of *tapas,* then all the sages should possess both, as the ancient sages did. We have known that the ancient sages had these *siddhis* and were also liberated at the same time. Why do not all *jñânis* possess such powers as well?

45. *Master:* Of the two types of *tapas,* namely, *tapas* for the fulfilment of one's desires,[21] and dispassionate *tapas*,[22] the former bestows the powers desired, and the latter wisdom. Each can yield its allotted fruits only. That is the law. The ancient sages had evidently performed both kinds of *tapas*.

46. Sinless son, Janaka, Mahâbali, Bhâgîratha and others got deliverance only. Did they display any *siddhis?* (No). Some of the sages sought *siddhis* only; others sought both *siddhis* and emancipation. These *siddhis* are simply for display and nothing more. They do not make for liberation.

47. *Disciple:* If emancipation be the sole outcome of the realization of identity of the individual self with the universal Self, how then did some of the sages,[23] who were liberated here and now, exert themselves for the attainment of *siddhis?*

Master: Prârabdha spends itself only after bestowing its fruits, to be experienced (as pain or pleasure). Therefore the *siddhis* gained by emancipated sages must be considered to be the results of *prârabdha* only.

19. E.g. fasting, prayers, rituals.
20. Meditation with control of breath, in particular postures.
21. *Sakâmya.*
22. *Nishkâmya*
23. E.g. *chûdâlâ* (vide *Yoga* Vasishtha*).*

48 & 49. *Disciple:* O Master who so graciously answers all my questions with holy texts and reasoning, so that my mind may remain unshaken, I am now free from the delusions of the mind[24] and remain pure and clear. There is certainly no harm in cleaning a mirror[25] a little more even though it is already clean.

O Lord who has removed my misery! Your words are like nectar and do not satiate. Can the scriptures say anything that is not absolutely true? Gracious Master, how can I reconcile the two statements: the *karma* of any person wears away only after bestowing its fruits; and the fire of pure wisdom burns away the *karma* which is waiting to bear fruits later on?[26]

50. *Master:* My son, the *jîva*s are unlimited (in number, capacity and kind), and their actions also are similarly unlimited. In three sections[27] the beneficent *Vedas* prescribe according to the aptitudes of seekers, with preliminary views succeeded by final conclusions,[28] like flowers by fruits.

51. Is it not true that sinners who must suffer in the hells, can yet be saved from them by means of pious gifts, *mantras,* austerities, *yajña* and the like? He who has faith in the saying of the *Vedas* that the fire of *jñâna* burns away all *karma* waiting to yield its results, attains liberation.

52. *Disciple:* Beloved Master who ever abides in the tabernacle of my heart! When true wisdom can root out the *karma* which has been accumulated in many incarnations, and liberate the person, why do even the most brilliant of men not profit by this wisdom, but fall into the rut of *karma* and perish? Please explain!

---

24. The delusions are of five kinds: (1) that the world is real; (2) that I am the body; (3) that I am the doer and the experiencer; (4) that I am separate from the Almighty; and (5) that pure Consciousness is not "I" but *Shiva.*
25. The ancient metallic mirror is meant here.
26. *Sanchita karma.*
27. *Karma, upâsana* and *jñâna.*
28. *Siddhânta.*

53. *Master:* My son, those of in-turned mind[29] will realize the everlasting "That". Like absent-minded walkers falling into a ditch even with their eyes open, those of outgoing mind look for the fulfillment of their desires, fall into the contemptible sea of never-ending rebirths and cannot gain liberation.

54. *Disciple:* Are not the good and bad actions actuated by *Îshvara?* What can the *jivas* do who are themselves His creatures? How are they to blame, worthy Master?

Master: My son, hear me! These are words of illusion, worthy of fools ignorant of the clear meaning of the scriptures.

55. The creations of the almighty Lord and of the individual *jîva* are different. The Almighty's creation is cosmic and consists of all that is mobile and immobile. The unworthy *jîva's* creation, which consists of attachments, passions, desires and the like, pertains to the ego and is certainly not of the Almighty.

56. The creations of the almighty Lord, who functions three-fold,[30] may constitute the means for liberation, whereas those of the *jîvas* are the maladies which cause them successive reincarnations. Liability to birth does not end for any one, even if creation comes to an end, but it ends on the giving up of one's passions and the like.

57. Whoever got free from rebirths at the time of the dissolution of the Lord's creation? (No one). Despite the persistence of time, space and bodies, people have been liberated even here, by destroying the illusion of individual creation, and gaining Knowledge. Therefore bondage and illusion are clearly of the *jîva's* own making and not of the Lord's.

58. There is a tree, called the *Ashvattha* and two birds live on it. One of them who is full of desires, enjoys the fruits, saying

29. i.e., those who look on diversity as an illusory phenomenon or those who consider *Brahman* to be the undivided Whole.
30. As the Creator, the Preserver and the Destroyer.

"This is sweet; this is sweet." The other, who is highly esteemed, does not eat thereof. Understand this parable by which the holy *Veda* describes the *jîva* and *Îshvara*.[31]

59. Those fools head for disaster who in their ignorance attribute to God the six evils,[32] which are of their own making, but the wise will gain untainted deliverance who recognise the same evils to be of their own making and not God's.

60. *Disciple:* O Master, who is bliss incarnate! How is it that God, who is impartial, advances a few and degrades others ?

Master: He is like the father who encourages his sons who are in the right way, and frowns on the other sons who are in the wrong way. Know it to be mercy to punish the erring and direct them to be righteous.

61. O son, whose fetters of worldly life are broken! The celestial tree,[33] fire and water, protect those who seek them by fulfilling their desires, keeping them warm and quenching their thirst. So also, *Îshvara* is kind to His devotees and not so to others. Now think well and judge whose fault it is.

62. Now, my son! Here is the vital point: Rebirths will be at an end for him who adopts with perseverance the way to Deliverance shown by God in the scriptures, follows the sages, gives up his evil propensities, discriminates the real from the

---

31. This parable is found in the *Mundaka-Upanishad.* The body is compared to a tree because it can be felled. Its roots are high in the holy *Brahman* and its branches are low, as the vital airs and the like. Its duration cannot be definitely ascertained and therefore it is called *Ashvattha* (i.e., not dependable), the holy fig tree. Its stay is coeval with *ajñâna* and therefore indeterminate. The *jîva*s require the body for experiencing the results of their *karma*. Hence it is said to be the *kshetra* (abode). In this dwelling place, there live the two birds, namely the ego and the universal Self who are respectively the experiencer and the unconcerned Witness.
32. viz., *kâma, lobha, moha, mada, krôdha, mâtsarya* (lust, anger, greed, delusion, conceit and jealousy).
33. *Kalpakarvrikshâ.*

unreal, rejects the illusion born of ignorance and gains Wisdom (by realizing the Self). Then, and then only, will rebirths be at an end for him. This is the Truth.

63. This Wisdom can be gained by a long course of practice of unceasing enquiry into the Self.
Disciple: What is this enquiry?

Master: Enquiry consists in pondering over the questions: Who is this I in the body, including mind, senses, etc.? What is sentience? What is insentience? What is their combination called bondage? What is release?

64. *Disciple:* The cumulative effect of all the meritorious actions of past births would confer *jñâna* on us. What is the need for an enquiry into the Self?

Master: Hear me! The unselfish actions which were rendered unto God help to keep off impurities, and make the mind pure. The mind which has thus been purified begins to enquire into the Self, and gains Knowledge.

65. *Disciple:* Holy Master! Is it not possible for rituals and other powerful actions—which confer devotion, dispassion, happiness in the other world, supernatural powers, steadfastness in austerities, success in *yoga*, meditation and divine form—to give right knowledge which removes illusion? What need is there for enquiry also?

66. *Master:* Hear me, son. If you want to identify the persons in a masquerade, you set about to discover their nature, habits and traits which are now hidden. If on the other hand, you run about, jump, turn somersaults, climb posts, dance and fuss about, that will not help you to recognize them.

67. Likewise, enquiry alone can lead to the knowledge revealed in the *Vedas*, which only point to *Brahman* indirectly.

Knowledge of the Self cannot be gained by a study of the *Vedas,* feeding the hungry, performing austerities, repeating *mantras,* righteous conduct, sacrifices and what not.

68. *Disciple:* O Master of crystal clear wisdom! The stain[34] on a shining mirror can be removed only by rubbing it. Or has anyone made it stainless by knowledge only? Similarly the dirt of ignorance should be removed by *karma.* How can it be done away with by knowledge which is only mental? Tell me.

69. *Master:* Son! The stain on a (metallic) mirror is material and also natural to it. But the black is not natural to the crystal (quartz), it is only superimposed on it. Appropriate work is doubtless necessary to remove the stain on the mirror. But to know that the black is a superimposition on the crystal, the mind alone will succeed.[35]

70. Here also, non-being,[36] insentience and misery are all superimposed on Being-Consciousness-Bliss by (the play of) *Mâyâ.* They are neither natural nor real. The series of *karma* does not conflict with *avidyâ* (ignorance) though it is perishable; on the contrary, it nourishes it. *Jñâna* (realization) is the fire which burns away *karma* and ignorance.

71. A man who has forgotten where he left his things in the house cannot recover them by weeping even for a hundred years. But he will get them only if he thinks the matter over and finds out. The Self is realized directly by Knowledge which destroys forgetfulness (ignorance), the root-cause of all misery, but it cannot be realized by any amount of hard work, though extended over several aeons.[37]

---

34. The mirror is metallic, and the stain is verdigris.
35. The master compares ignorance to the color transmitted by a clear crystal behind which a colored foil is set.
36. *Shunya:* blank, void.
37. *Yugas.*

72. *Disciple:* Master! Why should the *Veda,* which says that *jñâna* is the sole means of supreme Bliss, classify *karma,* in the *karma-kânda,* as merit, sin and a mixture of the two, which make the doers reincarnate as celestial beings, animals (beasts, birds, trees, insects and so on) and human beings respectively; and further prescribe special duties for different castes and orders of men as conferring happiness when properly done?

73. *Master:* Like the coaxing of a loving mother concerned with the sickness of her child who has eaten earth, and who offers it a tempting sweet in which a medicine is wrapped, the cheering statement of the *Vedas,* "Do your household duties; perform sacrifices; they are all good!" means something different. It is not understood by seekers of pleasure in heaven.

74. Look, it is only natural that pleasure-seekers eat what they get and embrace whom they can. Would the scriptures dictate what is after all natural to every one? Do they not know so much? No one need order: "Crow, be black! Fire, burn! Neem,[38] be bitter! You fleet wind, blow!"

75. When the *Vedas* enjoin: "If you desire fermented drinks and meat, have them by performing sacrifices; if you have a sexual impulse, embrace your wife," the person is expected to desist from other ways of satisfying his desires.

The *Vedas* aim at total renunciation only.

Disciple: In that case, why should there be these commandments at all?

Master: They are only preliminary[39] and not final.[40]

38. Margosa, or *azadirachta indica.*
39. *Pûrvapaksha.*
40. *Siddhânta.*

76. Note that the *Vedas* which advise thus: "Drink the fermented juice; eat the meat," say later on "smell it." Note also the commandment: "Desire sexual union for the sake of a child." Note again (the commandment): "Give up this also (i.e. sacrifice, marriage, wealth and other possessions)." Note further that complete renunciation is not a slur on a *sannyâsin* or a *brahmachâri*. Understand the scheme as a whole, give up any desire for action, and thus you will gain beatitude.

77. *Disciple:* O Master! Granting that actions simply aid the ignorance which gives rise to the world, if knowledge be inimical to ignorance which brings about this diversity, how can such ignorance co-exist with stainless Knowledge, like the spot in the moon, and effect these creations?

78. *Master:* O son! Consciousness which is Itself self-luminous has two aspects: pure Consciousness,[41] and modal consciousness.[42] The former manifests as the latter and they are not therefore exclusive of each other. You have known that pure Consciousness is not inimical to ignorance in deep sleep. Modal consciousness burns away ignorance, which rests on pure Consciousness.

79. *Disciple:* How can *Mâyâ*, which expands and contracts like a bellows, remain unaffected by pure Consciousness, but be burnt away by modal consciousness?

Master: See how the sun shines over the whole world and sustains it, yet becomes fire under a lens and burns. So also, in *samâdhi,* modal consciousness can burn away ignorance.

80. *Disciple:* Do not actions include all modes of mind, speech and body? Is not modal consciousness a function of the inner

---

41. *Svarûpa jñâna:* all-diffusive, static consciousness.
42. *Vritti jñâna:* directed or particularized consciousness. These two can be compared to the latent energy in fuel and burning fire which reduces it to ashes, or to electric current which remains unmanifest in a live wire and the same current which manifests as light in the filament of a bulb.

faculty? Then should we not say that action (a special mode of mind) destroys ignorance? Why is it marked off with the imposing title of Knowledge? Please explain me this.

81. *Master:* Modal consciousness is truly a mode of mind, but we have seen that the sons of the same mother fight among themselves.

Actions pertain to the doer, whereas knowledge born of enquiry, does not pertain to the individual,[43] but pertains to the thing in itself.[44]

82. The injunctions may be done, may not be done, or be done differently,[45] but Knowledge, which is paramount, cannot be so.

Meditation (such as "I am *Brahman*") is certainly different from Knowledge obtained by enquiry. To formulate one thing as another is forced *yoga.*[46] Direct knowledge[47] can alone be true. Do not be deceived by fanciful ideas.

83. Knowledge is the result of direct experience, whereas meditation is mere mental imagery of something heard. That which is heard from others will be wiped off the memory, but not that which is experienced. Therefore that which is experienced is alone real, but not those things that are meditated upon. Know that knowledge, but not *karma,* is the destroyer of ignorance at sight.

84. Do not doubt that unreal meditation can grant real final deliverance. Hear me! During meditation the image meditated

43. *Purusha tantra.*
44. *Vastu tantra*
45. Even the *nirguna Brahman dhyâna* may be done as prescribed, may be omitted, or may be done at the sweet will of the person. It is not intrinsic to the man as *jñâna* is to the thing in itself.
46. There are different kinds of *dhyâna.* In one of them, *sâligrâm* is meant to represent Vishnu, who is four armed, holding a conch, a discus, a club and a lotus. This *dhyâna* is forced but yet effective.
47. i.e., gained by experience.

upon by hearsay is not real, but when it is materialized and is seen face to face, it becomes real.[48]

85. If you ask how unreal meditation leads to real and ever-lasting deliverance: Each one is reborn in accordance with the last thought of his previous life.[49] Persons are reborn in the forms they meditated upon. But should one meditate upon the Self in order to do away with any kind of rebirth, then one becomes the Self. This is sure and certain.

86. *Disciple:* If those who meditate on attributeless (i.e., transcendental) *Brahman,*[50] become That, O Master in human form, where is the need for enquiry or for knowledge?

Master: Meditation upon *Brahman* is based on hearsay;[51] however, it becomes a fact of experience in due course. This experience is called the everlasting enquiry, knowledge or *jñâna* (which destroys ignorance), or deliverance. This is the final conclusion.[52]

87. *Disciple:* If modal consciousness[53] (after destroying ignorance) be left over in the all-perfect Self,[54] how can there be the experience of undivided being?[55]

Master: Just as cleansing-nut[56] powder carries down the impurities[57] in water, and settles down with them, so also modal consciousness destroys ignorance and perishes with it.

---

48. It follows that the "I am *Brahman*" of the contemplative stage is not real, but the resulting *experience* "I am *Brahman*" is real.
49. Vide *Shrimad Bhagavad Gîtâ,* Ch. VIII.
50. *Nirguna Brahman.*
51. *Paroksha.*
52. *Siddhânta.*
53. *Vritti jñâna.*
54. *Paripûrna.*
55. *Akhanda anubhâva siddhi.*
56. *Stychnos potatorum.*
57. Lit. *the mud.*

88. *Disciple:* Well, what is the nature of the wise, liberated here and now?

Master: They are free from thoughts and therefore live happy, like an undisputed suzerain of the whole world, or like a babe. The ideas of bondage and release vanish for them altogether, so much so that they laugh at those who speak of such things. For, are they not to be laughed at, who say that a mosquito took in the ether and vomited it forth?

89. The son of a barren woman and the man seen in the post[58] wore flowers gathered in the sky, wrangled over the price of the silver in mother-of-pearl,[59] in the city of the *Gandharvas*,[60] armed themselves with the horns of hares,[61] fought and stabbed each other, died together and turned into ghosts.

No man of sense will be excited on hearing this story.[62]

90. Since *Mâyâ* itself is unreal, all its creation must likewise be unreal. Can the progeny be of a different species from the mother?[63]

Therefore, do not heed heaven or hell, good or bad; but stay as the Self which is *sat-chit-ânanda-pûrna* (Perfection).

91. *Disciple:* My Lord! Tell me, is it not blasphemy to deny as unreal, the lotus-seated Creator and the other gods, the great

---

58. In dim light, a thick post is mistaken for a man. Such an illusory man is meant here. In a similar story *Yoga* Vasishtha mentions the reflected image of a man in a mirror.
59. The nacre of mother-of-pearl is mistaken for silver. This fancied silver is meant.
60. The *Gandharvas* are a class of celestial beings. At sunset, the clouds shine with gorgeous colours. In peculiar dispositions of such bright clouds, a fancy may sometime arise that it is the cheerful city of the happy *Gandharvas*.
61. They are non-existent.
62. The story starts with two non-existent men and indulges in mere fancy. The world and its activities are no more real to the *jñâni* than this story is to an average man.
63. E.g., can a mare bring forth a human being, an elephant or a bird?

men of the world, holy waters like the Ganges, the places of pilgrimage, the holy occasions, the four *Vedas* with their six auxiliaries,[64] the *mantras* and austerities?

92. *Master:* If it be sacrilege to deny dream-visions as false, it would be sacrilege too to deny the world[65] which derives its existence from illusion. If on the other hand it is right to deny dream-visions, it is only right to deny the world also which is derived from illusion.

93. If the *Purânas* hold up as men of merit, the ignorant who regard the false as true, does any *shâstra* attach censure to the *jñâni* for calling the truth?

Mâyâ, which appears as the elements and their modifications with different names and forms, is false. Only the Self which is all diffusive as *Sat-Chit-Ânanda,* is the Truth.

94. *Disciple:* O Master who is like a typhoon in dispersing the clouds of *Mâyâ!*

(a) Of what nature is *Mâyâ?* (b) Who are in its grip?

(c) How did it come into being? (d) Why did it arise?

(e) Duality is inevitable if *Mâyâ* is separate from *Brahman.*
If not separate, *Brahman* Itself is false (like *Mâyâ*).

95. *Master:* (a) Because its nature is not determinable, *Mâyâ* is said to be inexpressible.[66]

(b) They are in its grip who think: "This is mine," "I am the body," "the world is real."

(c) O Son, no one can ascertain how this mysterious illusion came into being.

(d) As to why it arose, it is because of the (person's) want of *vichâra* (discerning enquiry).

64. Such as *chandas, kalpa, jyotisha.*
65. With its contents.
66. *Anirvachaniya.*

96. *(e)* A magician's unseen powers remain unknown until hordes of illusory beings make their appearance in the show. Similarly the countless powers of *Brahman* remain unknown, but they are inferred only after the manifestation of the elements.

97. The magician who stands on *terra firma* and the hordes (conjured up by him) are visible to the onlookers. But his wonderful genius for magic remains mysterious. So also the handiwork of illusion (the world) and the wielder of illusion. There are many powers distinct from almighty *Brahman* and the world.

98. The power is not apart from the wielder. The wielder of magic is real, but the apparitions (of magic) are not. Wise son, you can from this illustration ascertain the true nature of the Reality which is the wielder of illusion and which at the same time remains whole and as the Self. Thus, get clear (of your doubts).

99. *Disciple:* Why should the power which is unreal, be said to exist?

Master: Good-natured son! Look how the grasses, and their like which appear insentient, put forth blossoms and bear crops. But for the consciousness pervading them, immobile beings would lose their immemorial nature.

100. See the wonder of how embryos in eggs develop into birds of so many hues! But for the governance of an unseen force, all (the laws of nature) would be blotted out, like a kingdom without a king. Fire would burn water; bitter things taste sweet; even the degraded would recite the *Vedas*; the immovable mountain ranges would float like clouds in the air; all the oceans would become sand wastes, and there would be no fixity anywhere.

101. *Disciple:* O Master who are the transcendent Reality! How can this power of Consciousness (i.e. *Mâyâ*), which cannot be seen or known or expressed by any one in words, and which

forms the root-cause of diverse names and forms, be rooted out? Otherwise, how is *Brahman* to be meditated upon as the non-dual Reality, to gain deliverance?

102. *Master:* What becomes of the well-known qualities of air, water or fire when they are checked by amulets or incantations? If you stay as *Sat-Chit-Ânanda*, free from other thought, *Mâyâ* becomes extinct. No other method can be found in the whole range of the *Vedas*.

103. What remains unmanifest in clay, becomes manifest (as a pot) and destroys it. To discard names and forms and recognize the clay, is true knowledge. In the same manner, discard the fancied notions of plurality of beings and realize the Self as pure Consciousness.

104. *Disciple:* Though false, how can the persistent appearance of non-being—insentience-misery in the fullness of Being-Consciousness-Bliss be wiped away?

Master: Though the reflection in the water appears head downwards and tremulous, yet when the figure on the ground is considered, which remains upright and steady, that worthless image is seen as only unreal.

105. Knowledge is the cause, and objects are the effects. It is fruitless to discuss how the phantoms of names and forms came into being and how they will vanish.

Worthy son! Not caring how this long-drawn out dream of the world came into being or how it is withdrawn, only remain aware as the Consciousness-Self which is all-embracing.

106. To the degree that you turn away from attachments to the unreal, your inner vision of Reality develops. If by a steady practice of this kind, the mind comes under control and becomes aware as Consciousness-Self, you can abide as the ocean of Bliss, though living in the bitter body.

107. *Disciple:* O Master! I do not see the propriety of the statement that all beings are permeated by the single non-dual Self which is all-embracing as Being-Consciousness-Bliss. The existence of the *jīvas* is clear because they all say "I"; Consciousness also is clear because of knowledge which is obvious; why does not Bliss show forth in a similar way?

108. *Master:* Son, although there are shape, fragrance and softness together present in the same flower, each of them is cognized by a separate sense only; otherwise they are not perceived. Such is the law of nature. Similarly, though the beatific qualities Being, Consciousness and Bliss together form the Self, yet the modes vary constantly and give rise to the differences which appear as the world.

109. My son! The three qualities—*sattva, rajas* and *tamas*—give rise to the three modes: repose, agitation and ignorance respectively. Being, Consciousness and Bliss, which are themselves glorious, always remain a homogeneous whole, yet appear different.

110. Bare existence alone is noticed in plants, minerals and the earth which look insentient and are ignorant.

There can be no happiness in the state of disturbance caused by passions, such as lust, which act like poison. But Being and Consciousness are evident in it.

Being, Consciousness and Bliss together become manifest in the state of Peace which is characterized by a stern detachment (from externalities).

Therefore Bliss becomes clear in a peaceful mind rid of ignorance and agitation.

111 . *Disciple:* Lord who has appeared as my Master in the world! I do not clearly understand the character of Being-Consciousness-Bliss *(Sat-Chit-Ânanda).* What is this *Sat?* What is *Chit?* And what is *Ânanda?*

Master: Sat (Being) is that which does not perish at any

time—past, present or future.

Chit (Consciousness) is that which cognizes the different objects.

Ânanda (Bliss) is the joy arising out of the experience of bliss during the enjoyment of an object of desire.

112. *Disciple:* O Master, who like an elephant in rut, attacks and demolishes the forts of the sheaths,[67] although the *mahâvâkyas* in the four *Vedas* declare, "Thou art *Sat-Chit-Ânanda*" to the indweller in the mortal body, and Masters say, "Thou art *Brahman*," yet how can one experience, "I am *Sat-Chit-Ânanda*"?

113. *Master:* When it is said that rebirths are the inevitable results of past actions, does it not follow that the person was existent in the past? Again, should heaven and hell be the rewards of present actions, does it not follow that he will continue to exist in the future? A subtle body (suited to heaven or hell), a celestial body or a human body, which are all the results of illusion, often change and pass away.

Always surviving the false body, it is but right to say that he is *Sat.*

114. In the darkness covering deep sleep and night, when there is no sun or lamp, he is unmistakably aware of darkness and objects, so he is *Chit.*

He is also *Ânanda* because his love never fades for the incomparably beatific Self; for love manifests only for an object of pleasure.

115. Food, drink and so forth are dear to all alike because pleasure is derived from them. The Self is not likewise a means to beatitude. Should the Self described above be classed along with other means of pleasure, where is the pleasure apart from the enjoyer thereof? Can the Self be two?

---

67. *Annamaya-kosha,* etc.

116. Love for sensual pleasure is evident, but the love for the Self remains unrivaled. The love for sensual pleasures undergoes changes whereas the intense love for the Self remains unchanging. Sensual pleasures can be enjoyed or rejected, but who is there to accept or reject the Self? The Self can reject all other pleasures but not reject Itself.

117. It is wrong to imagine that the Self kills Itself and gets rid of Itself by committing suicide in a burning passion. He who kills the body cannot be the body given up by him. The disgust is for the body and never for the Self.

118. Wealth is much sought after, but a son is dearer than wealth; one's own body is dearer than a son; the senses are dearer than the body; the life breath is dearer than the senses; and the Self is very much dearer than life itself. This Self is the essence and the other three selves—the secondary[68] (viz. the son), the illusory[69] (the body) and the acting[70] ones (the ego)—successively increase in importance.

119. At the time of one's death, the secondary self, namely the son, who succeeds to the father's estate, assumes prominence. At the time of nourishment, the illusory self, namely the body, is prominent. When a happy future life is desired, the acting self, i.e., the ego, becomes prominent. But in the state of liberation, the Self, to wit pure Consciousness, is paramount.

120. Even a tiger becomes a favorite when it is obedient, and a son is hated when he thwarts one. In this world, the things like straw, which are neither loved nor hated, are treated with indifference. But under no circumstances does the love of the stainless Self diminish for anyone.

Therefore, my son, investigate your true nature which is unbroken Bliss only and realize the Self!

68. *Gauna âtma.*
69. *Mithyâ âtma.*
70. *Karta.*

121. *Disciple:* Worshipful Master! How many kinds of *Ânanda* (Bliss) are there?

Master: There are three:

(1) *Brahmânanda* (which shines as Pure Consciousness, e.g., in sleep);

(2) *Vâsanânanda* (which is present in reminiscence); and

(3) *Vishayânanda* (which is the joy of gaining the desired object).

However others say that there are eight kinds of *Ânanda.* The above three cover the other five (of the eight). I shall nevertheless tell you all these eight[71]. Hear me.

122. (1) *Vishaya sukha:* the pleasure of sensual enjoyment;

(2) *Brahma sukha:* the bliss of dreamless sleep;

(3) *Vâsana sukha:* the remembrance of the above for a few minutes immediately after waking;

(4) *Âtma sukha:* the happiness which ensues on determining that the Self is the dearest of all dear things;

(5) *Mukhya sukha:* the bliss of *samâdhi* when the veil of ignorance is completely lifted;

(6) *Nija sukha:* the contentment which results from indifference;

(7) *Advitiya sukha:* the happiness of holding on to the Self to the exclusion of duality;

(8) *Vidyâ sukha:* the happiness that results from the enquiry into the Self in accordance with the scriptural texts.

---

71. They are: (1) objective delight, described later in v. 123; (2) delight in *Brahman,* in vv. 124-127; (3) reminiscent delight, in v. 128; (4) delight in Self, in vv. 95-107 and 164-166; (5) paramount delight, in v. 130; (6) natural delight, in v. 129; (7) non-dualist delight, in vv. 114,121 and 167; (8) delight of knowledge, at the end. *Sukha* is *Ânanda.*

123. My son, hear me describe their distinguishing characteristics. A man who is always exerting himself in the waking state, seeks rest on his bed, out of sheer exhaustion. Then his mind is well turned inwards and in that state it reflects the image of the Bliss of Consciousness which shines by Itself. The pleasure which he then experiences, represents objective pleasure.[72]

124. The person who, feeling objective pleasures poor because they involve the painful triads,[73] keeps the mind in repose and falls into sleep like an eagle dropping into its nest, becomes one with the limitless transcendent Being and remains as the blissful Self. This supreme state of Bliss is unrivalled *Brahmânanda.*

125. That the Bliss of deep sleep is *Brahmânanda* is the statement of the scriptures. That some persons take elaborate care to provide themselves with downy beds to sleep on, is the fact which supports it. That in that state all sense of right and wrong, of man or woman, of in or out, is totally lost, as at the time of the embrace of the beloved, is the experience which confirms it. So it is *Brahmânanda,* sure and certain.

126. *Disciple:* O Master, adored even by the gods! You are all-knowing and can kindly clear this doubt of mine: In this world of cause and effect, the experience of one cannot be felt by another. In deep sleep, the intellectual sheath has subsided and the blissful sheath has the experience of happiness. Is it right that this experience should be remembered by the intellectual sheath which expresses it?

127. *Master:* Know that these two (stand to each other in the relationship of) melted ghee and solidified ghee.

---

72. *Ânanda* has already been said to be the characteristic of *sattva guna* which is the state of repose. Therefore any shade of *Ânanda* must be traced to the mind which is free from agitation, even sensual pleasure.
73. The enjoyer, enjoyment and the object enjoyed.

They differ in their (limiting) thoughts, but not in their intrinsic knowledge. The intellectual sheath limited by the mind and active in the waking state, and the blissful one made of the bliss of pure Consciousness, which appears when the painful mind subsides in deep sleep, are not different from each other, just like rain-water and the water stored in a reservoir, or like sugar and syrup.

128. *Disciple :* In that case, why should any one lose hold of that non-dual bliss of *Brahman* and come out of it?

Master: He is drawn out by the force of his past *karma*. The man who has just wakened from deep sleep, does not immediately lose the happiness of sleep, for he does not bestir himself at once nor forget the happiness. This short interval of peace, which is neither sleep nor waking, is the Bliss of remembrance.

129. At the instant the "I-am-the-body" idea starts, he loses himself in the troubles of the world and forgets the bliss. His past *karma* brings on pain or pleasure. Peace results in equipoise. Everyone has experienced the state void of thoughts and the pleasure consequent upon it. This is *nijânanda*.

130. Can this be the bliss of *samâdhi*? (No). The external moisture is not the water contained within the pot. This happiness (of indifference) is only the shadow of the bliss of yogic *samâdhi* cast upon the rising ego. When the ego subsides and *samâdhi* results, there is the state of repose in which the mind is not aware of the environment, nor asleep, and the body stays stiff like a post.

131. Of the happiness enjoyed by the sole sovereign of the world, the earthly *Gandharvas* and celestial *Gandharvas*,[74] the brilliant *pitris*,[75] the gods existing from creation, the later gods

74. A class of celestial beings who enjoy music, dancing, etc.
75. The elders of the gods because they were created before them.

and celestial chiefs, Indra,[76] Brihaspati,[77] Prajâpati (or Virât),[78] Hiranyagarbha or (Brahmâ),[79] each is a hundred times as great as the preceding one. Yet all are fragmentary and like froth and form in the waters of the deluge of *Brahmânanda*.

132. Whosoever remains in the *turîyâtîta*[80] state, the seventh[81] (and the highest) plane, his experience of Consciousness-Bliss is the same as that of *Nârada, Shuka, Shiva,* Vishnu, *Brahmâ* and such others, free from duality or sleep. May the dust of his holy feet settle on my (humble) head!

133. So far I have now told you of five kinds of *Ânanda.* I shall later describe the bliss of Knowledge; I have already described the bliss of the Self[82] as the dearest of all and the bliss of the non-dual Self[83] while explaining *Mâyâ* and *Sat-Chit-Ânanda.* O Son, free from the pairs of opposites! Tell me, have you any more doubts?

134. *Disciple:* O Master that has created and preserves Lord Subrahmanya, myself and the whole cosmos, hear me!

If each of the terms *Sat, Chit* and *ânanda,* of which you have spoken, has characteristics of its own, how can the mind which is already unsteady be fixed (on Unity)? I do not see that they are different words with the same meaning. I pray you, kindly show me how it is all an indivisible, homogeneous whole like

76. The king of the celestials.
77. The preceptor of India.
78. The Creator of the gross world.
79. The root of the Creation.
80. Lit. *beyond the fourth.* The waking, dream and sleep states are the three which have their basis in the Self, so it is called the fourth in relation to the other three. But when the Self is realized as the sole Reality comprising all, there is no duality and related things. It is therefore absolute.
81. The spiritual planes are (1) *subhecchâ,* (2) *vichârana,* (3) *tanumânasi,* (4) *sattvâpatti,* (5) *asamshakti,* (6) *padârthabhâvani,* and (7) *turîyaga* (the transcendental state which is beyond description).
82. *Âtmânanda.*
83. *Advitiyânanda.*

honey which is uniform though gathered from different flowers by the bees.

135. *Master:* Is water tripartite because of its coldness, fluidity and whiteness (i.e., transparency)? Or is fire tripartite because of its light, heat and redness?

The *Vedas* have analysed and dismissed the cosmos beginning with the ether as unsubstantial, insentient and misery-laden. In contradistinction to this and for easy understanding they have described Brahman as *Sat-Chit-Ânanda*[84] which is One only.

136. The *Vedas* describe *Brahman* in affirmative terms as follows: Eternal, Whole, Unique, the highest Truth, the Supreme, the Repository, the Source, Peace, Ever-True, Absolute (continuum of the source, dream and sleep states, and therefore) the Fourth, Continuous or Equal in all, the Sight, the Witness of all, Knowledge, Pure, That which is indirectly denoted (by the *Vedas*), Everlasting, Indweller, the Reality, Ether, Light, the Self, Liberation, the Lord, Subtle, and so on.

137. In negative terms as: the Unmoving, Untainted, Immortal, Immeasurable, Unsullied, (That which is) beyond speech, the non-Insentient, the Diseaseless, Uncontaminated, Incomparable, Uninterrupted, Unattainable (by the mind or the senses), Undivided, Unborn, Infinite, Indestructible, (That which is) without qualities, Undivided, (That which is) without limbs or parts, Beginningless, Bodiless, Changeless, Non-dual, and so on.

138. When all these qualities, affirmative or otherwise, are considered together in the right way, they point to One only and there can be no other. Many may be the words to signify the same. Thus *Brahman*, signified by *Sat, Chit,* and *Ânanda* is One only. Realize this unity and remain as one undivided whole.

139. Do not say: "To describe *Brahman* by qualities is like

84. Being-Consciousness-Bliss.

speaking of a barren mother." Can there be any one so talented as to understand the nature of *Brahman* without being told? What the *Vedas* have revealed out of grace for gaining knowledge of *Brahman* and liberation in life, are not qualities of *Brahman* but *Brahman* Itself.[85]

140. *Disciple:* O Lord! Like millions of suns rising simultaneously, you have come forth as my Master to dispel the darkness of my ignorance! Hear me again.

In accordance with the statement of the *shrutis,* I have now understood beyond doubt that my Self is the indivisible Reality. If you will further establish it by arguments, the truth will be fixed in my mind like an iron spike driven into a living tree.

141. *Master:* Being must itself be Consciousness. If the Consciousness be different from Being, it must be nonexistent. How then can Being be revealed?

Again, Consciousness must itself be Being. If different from Consciousness, it must be insentient. The insentient cannot exist by itself. Thus Being and Consciousness, being identical, are also Bliss. This is the most agreeable argument (lit.: *seminal line of reasoning*). Otherwise, Bliss would be non-existent and insentient and there could be no experience of it (which is absurd).

142. How[86] is *Sat,* which exists at all times, revealed? By Itself or by another?

A: By another.

Q: Is that other non-existent or existent?

A: Non-existent.

Q: Fool! Can the son of a barren woman effect anything?[87]

---

85. Truth is ascertained by three kinds of proofs: *shruti, yukti* and *anubhâva.* Of these, *shruti* is dealt with in vv. 130-139, *yukti* from vv. 140-143, and *anubhâva* in v. 144.
86. The Master frames the questions and answers himself.
87. It is as absurd as the statement, "I am the son of a barren woman."

A: Then let it be something existing but different from the original *Sat.*

Q: How is its existence revealed? You must[88] say: "by another." Will there be an end to this chain of existent things and their cognizers? Your answer is therefore untenable, so get rid of this false reasoning.

143. Listen to experience agreeable to scripture and reason. Since the bliss of profound sleep persists as memory, this bliss itself must be knowledge. There was nothing besides it. Existing in the dissolution and deep sleep, you witness the darkness of ignorance. Now entering the heart, abide as the all-perfect Self!

144. In accordance with the teachings of the Master he himself realized that Being, Consciousness and Bliss are but the same Reality, which is homogeneous, like the honey that is gathered from different sources, and was long fixed in *samâdhi.* When he opened his eyes he realized himself to be the screen on which moves the kaleidoscopic picture composed of the mobile and immobile objects of the universe.

145. *Disciple:* O worthy Master after my own heart! Is there anything more for us to do than to have this unique experience? To think and speak of it, and to remain soaked with the experience, appears to be the only duty for sages. Be gracious and make clear to me how the previously mentioned (see v. 132) *turîyâtîta* or seventh plane of knowledge is the highest.

146. *Master:* After analysis the elders say that there are seven states of ignorance[89] and seven degrees of knowledge.[90] Of them all, first hear me mention the seven states of ignorance. The elders have named them thus:

88. In conformity with your previous answer.
89. *Ajñâna saptabhûmi.*
90. *Jñâna saptabhûmi.*

1. *Bîja-jâgrat:* the germinal state of waking;

2. *Jâgrat:* the waking state;

3. *Mâhâ-jâgrat:* the waking state firmly established;

4. *Jâgrat-svapna:* the state of day-dreaming, castles in the air;

5. *Svapna:* the dream state;

6. *Svapna-jâgrat:* cogitation of the dream after waking up from it; and

7. *Sushupti:* dreamless sleep.

147 & 148. 1. The germinal waking state is the uncompounded consciousness which rises up fresh from the unitary state of being.

2. The waking state contains the sprout of the ego which was previously absent from the germinal state.

3. The sprout of the "I" and "mine" which rises up with every birth, is the firm[91] waking state.

4. The fussy ego conjuring up visions is the dreaming wakeful state.

5. To have uncontrolled visions while sleeping after a full meal, is the state of dream.

6. To be thinking of the dreams after waking up from them, is the waking dream.

7. The dense darkness of ignorance is the state of deep slumber.

These are the seven states of ignorance. I shall now tell you the seven stages of knowledge which bestow liberation.

149. The elders have analysed them as:

1. *Subheccha:* desire for Truth;

---

91. Firm because it shows itself as often as it rises.

2. *Vichârana:* investigation into the Truth;

3. *Tanumânasi:* pure and attenuated mind;

4. *Sattvapatti:* the realization of the Truth;

5. *Asamshakti:* a detached outlook on the universe and its contents;

6. *Padârthabhâvani:* untainted awareness of Self;

7. *Turîyaga:* the highest and indescribable state.

150 & 151. 1. To wean away from unedifying associations and to desire knowledge of the Supreme is the first plane called *subheccha.*

2. To associate with enlightened sages, learn from them and reflect on the Truth, is called investigation.

3. To be free from desires by meditating on the Truth with faith, is the attenuation of the mind.

4. The shining forth of the highest knowledge in the mind owing to the development of the foregoing conditions, is realization.

5. To be free from illusion by firm realization of Truth, is the detached outlook on the universe.

6. The bliss of the non-dual Self, devoid of triads,[92] is untainted awareness of Self.

7. Sublime silence of the very nature of Self is *turîya.*

Hear why this seventh plane was said to be *turîyâtîta* (i.e., beyond the *turîya).*

152. The first three planes are said to be *jâgrat* (i.e., the waking state) because the world is perceived (in them as ever before).

The fourth plane corresponds to dream (because the world is recognized to be dreamlike).

Even the dim perception of the world gradually vanishes and therefore the fifth plane is called the sleep state.

Transcendental bliss prevails in the sixth which is therefore

---

92. Namely, the subject, the object and their link; i.e. the cognizer, the cognized and cognition.

called *turîya* (i.e., the fourth state, relative to the foregoing waking, dream and sleep states).

The plane beyond all imagination is the seventh one which the *Vedas* indicate as sublime silence (i.e., *turîyâtîta).*

153. Some sages consider the name *turîya*[93] to be in conflict with the foregoing explanation of *turîyâtîta* which, according to them, will be the glorious liberation after disembodiment.[94] In such a scheme, the sixth plane is the state of very deep slumber as compared with the dreamless sleep of the fifth plane.

I shall further tell you the peculiarities of these glorious planes.

154. Those who yet remain in the first three planes are practitioners and not emancipated.

Brahmavids are those who have gone into the fourth plane; they are pure and liberated.

Those in the next three planes are respectively *vara, varya,* and *varishta,* i.e., the eminent, the more eminent and the most eminent among the knowers of *Brahman.* I shall still further tell you the excellence of the planes of the enlightened.

155. Those who have remained in the first three planes and died before they reached the fourth plane, go to the happy regions; then they reincarnate and gradually gain liberation. They surely do not go to the unedifying lower planes.

O son! The first plane itself is difficult to gain. This gained, liberation is as good as gained.

156. If they gain the first or second planes of enlightenment in this world, even *mlecchas*[95] are as good as emancipated. By the holy feet of my Master, this is true! Cursed be they that deny it! Doubt not the *Vedas,* common to all. Strictly following the indicated way, clearly realize, "I am *Brahman*"!

93. Lit., *the fourth.*
94. *Videha-mukti.*
95. The *mlecchas* are those who deprecate the *Vedas.*

157. *Disciple:* O Lord who has taken me like rice out of paddy liable to sprout again! You have just said that the planes of knowledge lead even contemptible *mlecchas* to final liberation. But some say that liberation cannot be gained unless the person renounces all domestic ties and retires as a *sannyâsin.*[96] Please clear my confusion on this point.

158. *Master:* Son worthy of respect by the righteous! Your doubt is right. Hear me clear it. The renunciation which snaps domestic ties is of four kinds. They are: (1) *kuteechaka,* (2) *bahoodaka,* (3) *hamsa* and (4) *paramahamsa,* all of which are a panacea to the miseries of the World. But detachment and not the habiliments (ochre robes) is the sole requisite for such renunciation.

159. Detachment is again of three degrees according as it is dull, intense and very intense. That which is caused by a shock is impulsive and dull. Discarding home and wealth for life is the intense form. Disgust for *Brahmâloka* as being illusory is the very intense.

160 & 161. Dull detachment does not qualify one for *sannyâsa.*[97] Intense detachment makes the person eligible for the first two orders of *sannyâsa.* If strong and fit, he must move about as a *bahoodaka;* otherwise, he must stay (at one place) as a *kuteechaka.*

When detachment is very intense, he can take to the *hamsa* or *paramahamsa* order. They say that the *hamsa* cannot gain final liberation unless through *satyaloka*[98] whereas the *paramahamsa* can get it here and now. The *paramhansa* order which is so effi-

---

96. Here is the implication: *sannyâsa* is the fourth stage of life for a *brahmin.* He starts as a *brahmachâri* and learns the *Vedas;* then marries and becomes a *grihastha;* then retires as a *vânaprastha;* and lastly, renounces everything and becomes a *sannyâsin.* Some say that the *kshatriyas* are also eligible for *sannyâsa,* e.g., Raghu. Others say that the *vaishyas* too can take *sannyâsa,* but not the *shûdras* and the rest.

97. Because shock is the result of past sins whereas *sannyâsa* is the fruit of virtue.

98. i.e., *Brahmâloka,* to which he goes after death.

cient, is again of two grades.

162. A *paramahamsa* may be one who desires to know the Truth or is a realized being. The former is an intelligent practitioner in the first three planes. The latter is a remarkable and pure sage who is liberated here and now. The former class of *paramahamsa* is of two kinds. Here me speak of them also.

163. Of these, one will give up the ties of home (according to ritual), formally enter the order of *sannyâsa* and gain supreme knowledge.

The other kind, remaining as *brahmins, kshatriyas, vaishyas* and *shûdras,* gains supreme knowledge.

Knowing it from the *shâstras* and in actual practice, why do you still get confused? You must clear yourself by the authority of the *shrutis,* your own reasoning and immediate experience.

164. If birth be a fact, then death is inevitable. But I am *Brahman* who is never born. If I be that which is born, this "I" surely cannot be *Brahman.* Therefore, I am that "I" which is birthless and deathless *Brahman.*

165 & 166. Q: If I am *Brahman,* how does it happen that I do not know this "I"?

A: Who says "I" now?

Q: The intellect.

A: The intellect gets lost in a swoon. That which remains, never lost, as perfect Consciousness, is "I."

Q: This state of perfection is not clear to me. How can I experience it?

A: There is the experience of happiness in deep sleep, and it is "That." No happiness can be experienced anywhere when a want is felt. Therefore, the Self must be this perfection. This is the source of all.

167. The cosmos originated in the imagination of the mind. Reason shows that these worlds have their being in that

Consciousness. If the enquiry is pursued into the self as transcending all this and extending limitlessly, I remain as the one perfect Being.

168. *Disciple*: How should I remain, so that I may experience what you have described as Bliss?

Master: If you get rid of that mode of mind which gives rise to the states of waking, dream and sleep, you will remain as your true being and also experience Bliss.

169. If you ask how to control the activities of the mind, rising up from its latencies: Rule over the intellect and senses as your slaves. They will become extinct.

170. Also, by gentle control of the breath which blows like a bellows, the activities of the mind cease. If you are not inclined to practice this *yoga*, they will cease if you root out the massive ignorance of the causal body. Then too the mind stops its activities.

171. *Disciple*: By what means can I root out ignorance, the causal body?

Master: The *shrutis* can never mislead one. How can there be ignorance if you firmly fix their teaching in your mind: "I am the all-perfect being in whom the worlds appear"?

172. *Disciple*: How can I remain thus, when I engage in worldly transactions with a wandering mind?

Master: There is nothing apart from Me. Whatever is seen, is of Me. I am He who is Consciousness, and which sees all of this as being fictitious as my dream.

173. If you always remain aware that "I" am perfect Consciousness, what does it matter how much you think, or what you do? All this is unreal like dream-visions after waking. I am all-Bliss!

174-177. *Disciple:* I had in my countless past incarnations mistaken the body for the Self. High or low, seeing all as a mirage, I have by the grace of my Master realized the Self as "I" and been liberated.

What meritorious work have I done? I cannot describe my good fortune. I am blessed by the grace of my Master, Nârâyana of *Nannilam*! In my ecstasy I throw up my cloth in the air, and dance for joy!

How noble have my parents been that they named me Tândava (dancer), as if they even then foresaw that I would be overpowered by the joy of having realized the Self and therefore dance in ecstasy!

Before whom shall I pour forth this ecstatic bliss of mine? It rises from within, surges up, fills the whole universe and floods unbounded!

I bow to the lotus feet of the Almighty, who was so gracious as to bring me into contact with the Master who could teach me the Truth according to the holy texts!

178 & 179. Such is *vidyânanda*. Those who study this work with devotion will realize the high state of repose and be liberated here and now. In order that all may understand clearly *vidyânanda*, the true spirit of the Holy books, in Nannilam, Master Nârâyana appeared in my *samâdhi* and commanded me to make this *Kaivalya Navaneeta* perfect in every detail, and free from defect.

180. Through the grace of his Lord, Tândavesa has shown how, freeing oneself from the interior and the exterior, one may be converted into the One; and having been convinced that the intended sense of the *Vedas*, which are beyond thought, is "I," and that the body and such are but modes of sound *(nâda),* one may become the seer of all and see everything in oneself.

181. Those who, without wavering, recognize the one Witness of blazing lustre—*turîyâtîta*, which is perfected in the meaning of those three most excellent words: "That thou art"—will

unravel the knot of differences, and overcoming every obstacle, will be themselves converted into the Self.

182. This is the "delight of knowledge" spoken of by the *Vedas*. Those who worship the feet of Nârâyana, who has described it, are without blemish; those who, through the teacher of this pupil, approach the stage in which doubt is finished and steadily go forward to perfection, will obtain spotless emancipation.

183. The author has, through the two parts of this work, kindled the sublime light of the Spirit, to the end that the eternal darkness of *Mâyâ* may perish and, clearing all doubts rising from mental knowledge, which is affected by difference, has subjected the disciple to himself.

184. Praise, praise to the author of my salvation! He placed on his head the foot of Nârâyana, the Infinite Lord, who had made him his slave, and who, by means of the process of negation had destroyed what through imposition had arisen as a mere fictitious appearance, and put me in such a condition that I, with eyes of grace, can remain forever the spectator.

185. Just as the refreshingly cool water from the holy feet of one's wise Master sprinkled on one's head confers all the merits obtained from all the holy places of pilgrimage, so also the learners of this unique work acquire the merits of all the holy books and live as sages in the world.

APPENDIX I

No. The Planes of Enlightenment	I Scheme	Remarks	II Scheme Remarks
I. Subhecchâ II. Vichâranâ III. Tanumânasi IV. Sattvapatti	*Jâgrat* (the waking state) among the *jñâna-bhûmikas* *Svapna* (dream)	Because the world is perceived in them as ever before. Because the Reality underlying the world is realized and the world itself appears like a phantom.	
V. Asamshakti	*Sushupti* (sleep)	The darkness of ignorance is totally lost and therefore it corresponds to sleep in the planes of enlightenment.	
VI. Padârtha bhâvanî	Dense *sushupti*	There is no place for the cognizer, the cognized and cognition. The person cannot himself wake up from this state unless external influences draw him out forcibly.	*Turîya*: Because it is the fourth in relation to the three previous states.
VII. Turîyâ	Sublime silence	Existence as the Self only, whether manifest or unmanifest.	
VIII. Turîyâtita	*Videha-mukti*	The state of Liberation after disembodiment.	*Turîyâtita*: That which lies beyond the *turîya*. Not taken into account because there is nothing to speak of.

APPENDIX II

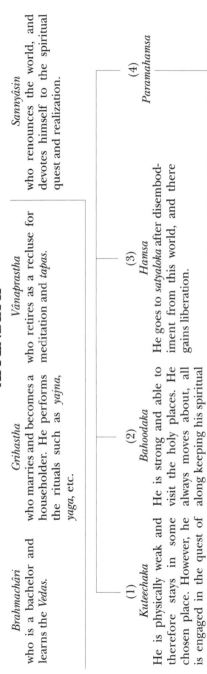

Brahmachāri

who is a bachelor and learns the *Vedas*.

Grihastha

who marries and becomes a householder. He performs the rituals such as *yajna*, *yaga*, etc.

Vānaprastha

who retires as a recluse for meditation and *tapas*.

Sannyāsin

who renounces the world, and devotes himself to the spiritual quest and realization.

(1)
Kuteechaka

He is physically weak and therefore stays in some chosen place. However, he is engaged in the quest of Truth.

(2)
Bahoodaka

He is strong and able to visit the holy places. He always moves about, all along keeping his spiritual quest in view.

(3)
Hamsa

He goes to *satyaloka* after disembodiment from this world, and there gains liberation.

(4)
Paramahamsa

or a *jñāni*, i.e., a realized sage. He is liberated here and now.

Jijñāsu, i.e., one who is desirous of knowing the Truth,

an informal *sannyāsi*, who is, however, highly developed, and therefore does not care for rituals and formality. He may be of any caste, or even a *mleccha*.

a formal *sannyāsi* who observes rituals. He is always a *brahmin* only.

(1) & (2) These two orders are for persons who are detached from the ties of home. Their detachment is of the middling quality.

(3) & (4) These two orders of *sannyāsa* are only for those whose detachment is of the noblest kind, i.e., ingrained and true. They do not care for anything but the Truth.

179

A Glossary of Terms
for *Advaita Bodha Deepika* and *Kaivalya Navaneeta*

(For a glossary of all key foreign words used in books published by World
Wisdom, including metaphysical terms in English, consult:
www.DictionaryofSpiritualTerms.org.
This on-line Dictionary of Spiritual Terms provides extensive definitions,
examples and related terms in other languages.)

âchârya: a teacher or spiritual Master; learned in philosophy and realized in knowledge (*jñâna*).

adhyâropa: lit. "false covering"; superimposition of the unreal upon
the real.

adhyâsa: false perception; superimposition.

advaita: non-duality; see *Vedânta*.

ahankâra: the ego; the "I"-consciousness.

ânandamaya-kosha: the sheath of bliss; see also *pañchakoshas*.

annamaya-kosha: the sheath of nutriment; the physical body; see also
pañchakoshas.

antahkarana: the internal organ, consisting of (1) mind (*manas*), (2)
memory (*chitta*), (3) intellect (*buddhi*), and (4) ego (*ahankâra*).

aparoksha: direct, immediate; see also *paroksha*.

apavâda: de-superimposition; the removal of superimposition.

arûpa: formless; beyond form; see also *rûpa*.

asamshakti: non-attachment; the fifth of the seven stages of enlightenment; see *Kaivalya Navaneeta* (*KN*), Appendix I.

âshrama: the four stages of life for a Hindu: *brahmacharya* (life as a
student), *grihastha* (life as a householder), *vânaprastha* (life as a forest-dweller), and *sannyâsa* (life as a renunciate); also a retreat, pri-
vate home, or monastery where spiritual seekers reside.

ashtânga-yoga: lit. "eight-limbed yoga"; a reference to the eight steps
of *râja-yoga*.

Âtma-jñâni: one who has realized the Self.

Âtman: the deepest essence of the being; the Supreme Self; identical
with *Brahman*; see *mahâvâkyâs*; also a reflexive pronoun that can
refer to any level of the being (i.e. to the body, vital breath, ego,
mind, intellect, etc.).

Âtma-vichâra: enquiry into the Self.

âvarana: the veiling or concealment of *Brahman* by manifestation.

181

avasthâ: state of consciousness; *Vedânta* distinguishes four planes of consciousness: (1) *jâgrat* (the waking state); (2) *svapna* (the dream state); (3) *sushupti* (the dreamless state of deep sleep); and (4) *turîya* ("the fourth," which transcends the three previous planes of consciousness).

avidyâ: ignorance.

avyakta: hidden, unmanifest.

bahoodaka: a wandering renunciate (*sannyâsin*) who undertakes pilgrimages to the holy sites; see *KN*, Appendix II; see also *kuteechaka, hamsa,* and *paramahamsa.*

Bhagavad Gîtâ: lit. "the Song of the Lord"; a text of primary rank dealing with the converse of *Krishna* (an incarnation of Vishnu) and the warrior *Arjuna* on the battlefield of *Kurukshetra.*

Bhagavân: noble; holy; an epithet used by devotees when addressing the personal God (*Îshvara*); also used in addressing a great saint.

bhakti-yoga: the spiritual path of love and devotion.

bhedavâsana: latencies connected with differentiation; see also *vâsana.*

bhogavâsana: latencies connected with enjoyment; see also *vâsana.*

brahmachâri: a celibate student; the first stage of life (*âshrama*) wherein a study of the scriptures is undertaken; see *KN*, Appendix II; see also *grihastha, vânaprastha,* and *sannyâsin.*

Brahmâloka: the heavenly paradise of *Brahmâ.*

Brahman: Absolute Reality; see also *nirguna Brahman* and *saguna Brahman.*

brâhmana: the educated priestly caste, including also: philosophers, scholars and religious leaders; see also *varna.*

Brahmavid: one who has realized *Brahman*; among the ones who have realized *Brahman*, those more eminent than the *Brahmavid* include (in ascending order): *Brahmavid-vara, Brahmavid-varya,* and *Brahmavid-varishta.*

Brihaspati: a *Vedic god*; chief priest of the gods.

buddhi: intellect; discriminative intelligence.

chandâla: outcaste or "untouchable"; pariahs who stand outside the caste system; see also *varna.*

darshana: lit. "viewing"; a name for the six classical schools of orthodox (*âstika*) Hindu philosophy: (1) *Nyâya* (logic); (2) *Vaisheshika* (natural philosophy, or science); (3) *Sânkhya* (cosmology); (4) *Yoga* (science of union); (5) *Pûrva-Mîmâmsâ* (meditation); and (6) *Uttara-Mîmâmsâ* (*Vedânta*, or metaphysics); also the blessing derived from beholding a saint.

dehavâsana: latencies connected with the body; see also *vâsana.*

182

deva: a god.

dvaita: duality.

Gandharvas: celestial musicians.

grihastha: a householder; the second stage in life (*âshrama*) wherein the student marries, performs the requisite rituals and serves family and community; see *KN*, Appendix II; see also *brahmachâri*, *vânaprastha*, and *sannyâsin*.

gunas: the three cosmic qualities of *sattva* (purity), *rajas* (passion), and *tamas* (obscurity) of which all of manifestation is constituted.

guru: spiritual guide or Master.

hamsa: a renunciate (*sannyâsin*) who attains to *Satyaloka* after the death of the body, there to obtain liberation; see *KN*, Appendix II; see also *kuteechaka, bahoodaka,* and *paramahamsa*.

Hiranyagarbha: a manifestation of *Îshvara* in association with the totality of subtle beings in the dream state; see also *svapna*.

Îshvara: lit. "the Lord of the Universe"; the personal God who manifests in the triple form of *Brahmâ* (the Creator), Vishnu (the Sustainer), and *Shiva* (the Transformer); identical with *saguna Brahman*.

jagat: the universe; the manifest world.

jâgrat: the waking state; associated with *vishva* and *annamaya-kosha*.

jîva: the individual soul; the living being.

jîvan-mukta: one who is liberated while still alive in the body.

jîvan-mukti: the state of liberation while still alive in the body.

jîvâtman: the individual self.

jñânendriya: the organs of sense-knowledge.

jñâna: knowledge; wisdom.

jñâna-kânda: the wisdom portion of the *Vedas*; see also *karma-kânda*.

jñâna-yoga: the spiritual path of knowledge or wisdom.

kaivalya: the state of liberation, or emancipation.

kârana-sharîra: the causal body; identical with *ânandamaya-kosha*.

karmendriya: the organs of action.

karma: action; the effects of past actions; the law of cause and effect ("as a man sows, so shall he reap"); of three kinds: (1) *sanchita karma*: actions of the past that have yet to bear fruit in the present life; (2) *prârabdha karma*: actions of the past that bear fruit in the present life; and (3) *âgâmi karma*: actions of the present that have still, by the law of cause and effect, to bear fruit in the future.

karma-kânda: the ritual portion of the *Vedas*; see also *jñâna-kânda*.

karma-yoga: the spiritual path of action.

karunâ: compassion.

kshatriya: the royal and warrior caste, including also: politicians, officers, and civil authorities; see also *varna*.

kuteechaka: a resident renunciate (*sannyâsin*) who remains fixed to one abode; see *KN*, Appendix II; see also *bahoodaka*, *hamsa*, and *paramahamsa*.

lokavâsana: latencies connected with the world; see also *vâsana*.

mahâvâkyâs: four "great sentences" from the *Vedas*, proclaiming the truth of *Âtman/Brahman* identity; they are: (1) *prajñanam Brahman* ("Consciousness is *Brahman*"); (2) *aham Brahmâsmi* ("I am *Brahman*"); (3) *tat tvam asi* ("thou art That"); and (4) *ayamâtman Brahman* ("this *Âtman* is *Brahman*").

maitri: benevolence; kindness.

manana: constant reflection upon the Truth as given by a spiritual Master (*guru*); the second of the steps towards *Vedântic* realization of the Self (*Âtman*); see also *shravana* and *nididhyâsana*.

manas: mind.

manomaya-kosha: the sheath of the mind; see also *pañchakoshas*.

manonasha: extinction of the mind.

mâyâ: cosmic illusion; the power (*shakti*) inherent in *Brahman* by which it manifests the world.

mleccha: foreigner; "barbarian"; one who deprecates the *Vedas*; see also *varna*.

moksha: liberation from *samsâra*; deliverance from ignorance (*avidyâ*).

Mt. Meru: in *Purânic* legend, the mythical golden mountain; the axis of the world.

muditâ: sympathetic joy; joy at the happiness of others.

mumukshutva: the desire for liberation; one of the four prerequisites for qualification as a spiritual aspirant of *Vedânta*; see *sâdhanâ-catushtaya*; see also *viveka*, *vairâgya*, and *shatkasampatti*.

nididhyâsana: meditation and contemplation upon the Truth as given by a spiritual Master (*guru*); the third of the steps towards *Vedântic* realization of the Self (*Âtman*); see also *shravana* and *manana*.

nirguna Brahman: lit. "*Brahman* without qualities"; *Brahman* as the Absolute and Infinite Reality (beyond all limiting words); see *saguna Brahman*.

nirvikalpa samâdhi: absorption in *Brahman* where all consciousness of duality or multiplicity is extinguished; see also *savikalpa samâdhi*.

padârthâbhâvani: the untainted awareness of the Self (*Âtman*); the sixth of the seven stages of enlightenment; see *KN*, Appendix I.

pañchakoshas: the five sheaths; *Vedânta* teaches that the Supreme Self

(*Âtman*), in manifesting itself in a *jîvâtman*, becomes enveloped in a series of five sheaths, namely: *ânandamaya-kosha*, *vijñânamaya-kosha*, *manomaya-kosha*, *prânamaya-kosha*, and *annamaya-kosha*.

paramahamsa: a renunciate (*sannyâsin*) who attains to liberation in this life; see *KN*, Appendix II; see also *kuteechaka*, *bahoodaka*, and *hamsa*.

paroksha: indirect, mediate; see also *aparoksha*.

pitris: ancestors.

Prajâpati: lit. "Lord of creatures"; the forefather of all beings.

prâjña: the individual being in the state (*avasthâ*) of deep sleep wherein the activity of the mind temporarily ceases and an unconscious, but fleeting, union with *Brahman* occurs; see also *sushupti*.

prajñâ: wisdom; pure consciousness.

prâna: vital breath.

prânamaya-kosha: the sheath of the vital breath; see also *pañchakoshas*.

râja-yoga: the principal system of yoga as taught by *Patañjali*, consisting of eight steps: (1) *yama* (self-control, by the practice of *ahimsa* [non-injury], *satya* [truth], *asteya* [non-stealing], *brahmacharya* [celibacy], and *aparigraha* [non-acceptance of gifts]); (2) *niyama* (restraint, by the practice of *shaucha* [cleanliness], *santosha* [contentment], *tapas* [austerity], *svâdhyâya* [self-study of the scriptures], and *îshvara-pranidhâna* [devotion and surrender to the personal God]); (3) *âsana* (bodily postures); (4) *prânâyâma* (breath control); (5) *pratyâhâra* (withdrawal of the senses); (6) *dhâranâ* (concentration of the mind); (7) *dhyâna* (meditation); and (8) *samâdhi* (non-dual consciousness of *Brahman*); equivalent to *ashtânga-yoga*.

Râma: the seventh incarnation (*avatâra*) of Vishnu and the hero of the epic tale the *Râmâyana*.

rûpa: form; see also *arûpa*.

sâdhaka: a spiritual aspirant; one who endeavors to follow a method of spiritual practice.

sâdhanâ: a method of spiritual practice.

sâdhanâ-catushtaya: the four prerequisites for qualification as a spiritual aspirant of *Vedânta*; they are: *viveka* (discrimination), *vairâgya* (dispassion), *shatkasampatti* (the six virtues), and *mumukshutva* (desire for liberation).

sâdhu: ascetic; also sage.

saguna Brahman: lit. "*Brahman* with qualities"; *Brahman* with "limiting" attributes such as Creator, Sustainer and Transformer; equivalent to the personal God (*Îshvara*); see also *nirguna Brahman*.

sâksatkâra: direct realization.

samâdhi: absorption in *Brahman*; see also *nirvikalpa samâdhi* and *savikalpa samâdhi*.

samsâra: the cycle of births and deaths; the phenomenal world.

sannyâsin: a renunciate; the fourth stage in life (*âshrama*) wherein the forest-dweller renounces the world and directs all effort towards liberation; see *KN*, Appendix II; see also *brahmachâri*, *grihastha*, and *vânaprastha*.

Satsanga: lit. "the company of the true"; association with spiritual persons.

sattvâpatti: the realization of Truth; the fourth of the seven stages of enlightenment; see *KN*, Appendix I.

Satyaloka: the heavenly paradise of pure Truth.

savikalpa samâdhi: absorption in *Brahman* where the consciousness of duality and multiplicity still remains; see also *nirvikalpa samâdhi*.

Shankarâchârya: an illustrious ninth century (C.E.) Hindu sage, philosopher and saint; the greatest of the exponents of the perspective of *Advaita Vedânta* through his learned commentaries on the *Upanishads, Brahma-Sutras*, and *Bhagavad Gîtâ*; also wrote introductory texts to the perspective of *Advaita Vedânta* such as *Viveka Chûdâmani* and *Âtma-Bodha*, and composed several devotional hymns to the goddess; see also *Vedânta*.

sharîra: body.

shâstras: legal textbooks which codify the laws governing Hindu civil society (*Mânava-Dharma-Shâstra*) and canonize the rules for the sacred arts of dance, music, drama, and sculpture (*Bharata-Nâtya-Shâstra*); also used more broadly to encompass the *Vedas* and all scriptures in accord with them; see also *shruti* and *smriti*.

shatkasampatti: the six great virtues, viz. (1) *shama*: control of the mind; (2) *dama*: control of the sense organs; (3) *uparati*: cessation of activities related to caste, creed, family etc.; (4) *titikshâ*: patient forbearance of suffering; (5) *shraddhâ*: faith in the holy scriptures and trust in the spiritual Master (*guru*); and (6) *samâdhâna*: concentration and contemplation upon the *Vedântic* texts and the words of the spiritual Master (*guru*); one of the four prerequisites for qualification as a spiritual aspirant of *Vedânta*; see *sâdhanâ-catushtaya*; see also *viveka, vairâgya*, and *mumukshutva*.

shravana: hearing the Truth from a spiritual Master (*guru*); the first of the steps towards *Vedântic* realization of the Self (*Âtman*); see also *manana* and *nididhyâsana*.

Shri: lit. "splendor, beauty, venerable one"; an honorific title set before the name of a deity or eminent human being; also a name of *Lakshmî*, the consort of Vishnu and the goddess of beauty and good fortune.

shruti: scriptural texts of divine revelation, including the *Samhitâs*, the *Brâhmanas*, the *Âranyakas*, and the *Upanishads*; see also *Vedas* and *smriti*.

shûdra: the laboring caste; see also *varna*.

smriti: classical texts that perpetuate and prolong the scriptural texts of divine revelation (*shruti*), including the *Upavedas* ("branches of the *Vedas*"), the *Vedângas* ("limbs of the *Vedas*"), the *shâstras* (classical "textbooks"), the *Purânas* (mythological tales), and the epic *Râmâyana* and *Mahâbhârata*.

sthula-sharîra: the gross body; identical with *annamaya-kosha*.

subheccha: the desire for Truth; the first of the seven stages of enlightenment; see *KN*, Appendix I.

sukshma-sharîra: the subtle body; identical with *prânamaya-kosha*, *manomaya-kosha*, and *vijñânamaya-kosha*.

sushupti: the dreamless state of deep sleep; associated with *prâjña* and *ânandamaya-kosha*.

svapna: the dream state; associated with *taijasa* and the *prânamaya-*, *manomaya-*, and *vijñânamaya-koshas*.

Swâmi: a title of respect set before the names of monks and spiritual teachers.

taijasa: the individual being in the dream state (*avasthâ*); see also *svapna*.

tanumânasi: the state of pure, attenuated mind; the third of the seven stages of enlightenment; see *KN*, Appendix I.

turîya: lit. "the fourth"; the state of consciousness which transcends the waking (*jâgrat*), dream (*svapna*), and dreamless sleep (*sushupti*) states; the state of pure Consciousness (*Chit*); also the final of the seven stages of enlightenment; see *KN*, Appendix I.

turîyâtîta: beyond "the fourth" (turîya); the supreme state of the Self (*Âtman*).

upadesha: instruction; teaching.

upâdhi: limiting attribute; in *Advaita Vedânta*, a reference to all names and forms (*nâma-rûpa*) that limit or conceal *Brahman*.

Upanishads: the last portion of the *Vedas*; the philosophical and metaphysical essence of the *Vedas*; see also *Vedânta*.

Upavedas: secondary texts that correspond to the four *Vedas* and which deal with such topics as medicine (*Âyur-Veda*), military science (*Dhanur-Veda*), music (*Gandharva-Veda*), and mechanics and architecture (*Sthâpatya-Veda*).

upekshâ: disregard of the faults of others.

vairâgya: dispassion; non-attachment; one of the four prerequisites for qualification as a spiritual aspirant of *Vedânta*; see *sâdhanâ-catushtaya*; see also *viveka, shatkasampatti,* and *mumukshutva.*

vaishya: the merchant caste, including farmers and providers; see also *varna.*

vânaprastha: a forest-dweller; the third stage in life (*âshrama*) wherein the householder retreats to the forest and undertakes philosophical study and meditational practice; see *KN,* Appendix II; see also *brahmachâri, grihastha,* and *sannyâsin.*

varna: caste; class; the four major social divisions in Hindu society include (in descending order): *brâhmanas* (priests), *kshatriyas* (royals and warriors), *vaishyas* (merchants and farmers), and *shûdras* (servants and laborers); situated outside the caste system are the *chandâlas* (outcastes and "untouchables") and *mlecchas* (foreigners and "barbarians"); members of the three upper castes are called "twice-born" (*dvija*) and are permitted to study the *Vedas.*

vâsânas: latent tendency; hidden desire; habit of mind; see also *lokavâsana, dehavâsana, bhogavâsana, vishayavâsana, viparîtavâsana,* and *bhedavâsana.*

Vedângas: lit. "limb of the *Veda*"; auxiliary sciences of the *Veda*, including astronomy, astrology, etymology, exegesis, grammar, euphony, and prosody.

Vedânta: lit. "the end of the *Veda*"; a designation for the *Upanishads* as the last portion ("end") of the *Vedas*; also one of the six orthodox (*âstika*) schools of Hindu philosophy who have their starting point in the texts of the *Upanishads,* the *Brahma-Sutras* (of *Bâdarâyana* Vyâsa), and the *Bhagavad Gîtâ*; over time *Vedânta* crystallized into three distinct schools: *Advaita* (non-dualism), associated with *Shankara* (ca.788-820 C.E.); *Vishishtâdvaita* (qualified non-dualism), associated with *Râmânuja* (ca.1055-1137 C.E.); and *Dvaita* (dualism), associated with *Madhva* (ca.1199-1278 C.E.).

Vedas: the sacred scriptures of Hinduism; regarded by the orthodox (*âstika*) as divine revelation (*shruti*) and comprising: (1) the *Rig, Sâma, Yajur,* and *Atharva Samhitâs* (collections of hymns); (2) the *Brâhmanas* (priestly treatises); (3) the *Âranyakas* (forest treatises); and (4) the *Upanishads* (philosophical and mystical treatises); they are divided into a *karma-kânda* portion dealing with ritual action and a *jñâna-kânda* portion dealing with knowledge.

vichârana: the enquiry into Truth; the second of the seven stages of enlightenment; see *KN,* Appendix I.

videha-mukta: one who is liberated after the death of the body.

videha-mukti: the state of liberation after the death of the body.

Vidyâranyaswâmi: an influential fourteenth century (C.E.) exponent of the perspective of *Advaita Vedânta*; author of the important *Advaitic* texts *Pañchadashi* and *Jîvanmukti-Viveka*.

vijñânamaya-kosha: the sheath of the intellect, or discriminative intelligence; see also *pañchakoshas*.

vikshepa: the projection or superimposition of manifestation upon *Brahman*, just as the concept "snake" is (falsely) projected upon a rope when seen in semi-darkness.

viparîtavâsana: latencies connected with wrong identity of self; see also *vâsana*.

Virât: a manifestation of *Îshvara* in association with the totality of gross beings in the waking state; see also *jâgrat*.

vâsanâksaya: extinction of the latent tendencies; see also *vâsana*.

vishayavâsana: latencies connected with the objects of sense; see also *vâsana*.

vishva: the individual being in the waking state (*avasthâ*); see also *jâgrat*.

viveka: discrimination between the eternal and the non-eternal; one of the four prerequisites for qualification as a spiritual aspirant of *Vedânta*; see *sâdhanâ-catushtaya*; see also *vairâgya*, *shatkasampatti*, and *mumukshutva*.

vritti: a mode or modification of the mind.

yoga: union with *Brahman*; also a spiritual path or practice; see *karma-yoga*, *bhakti-yoga*, *jñâna-yoga*, and *râja-yoga*.

Yoga Vasishtha: a text attributed to the poet *Vâlmîki* relating the spiritual instruction given by the sage Vasishtha to prince *Râma*; an expression of the perspective of *Advaita Vedânta*.

yogi: a practitioner of *yoga* (feminine: *yogini*).

INDEX

Index